Ambrose Panico

Solution Tree

Behave Yourself!

Helping Students Plan to Do Better

Foreword by Richard L. Curwin

D1223967

Acknowledgments

I know that my wife, Debbie, always believed my message to be significant; when I had second thoughts, she thought for me. My mother, Mary Angelina, straightened me out if I had third thoughts. My sons Ambrose and Andrew provided an example of what can be accomplished through hard work and acceptance of personal responsibility; their actions motivated me to act.

My assistant Suemarie Gonzalez kept me organized and focused when the daily grind made thinking clearly a real challenge. My colleagues Shannon Horton, Mary Pels, and Victoria Williams offered creative ideas and formats for securing information from students and parents, and provided the leadership required to facilitate teacher teams using this information to develop viable individual student intervention plans. The feedback they provided kept me real and did much to make this book relevant to real teachers in real classrooms. My editor, Caroline Wise, knows this book is my baby; I know she is the godmother. Caroline is a big part of why the book is so easy to read and apply.

Thank you,

Ambrose

Visit **go.solution-tree.com/behavior**
to download all of the reproducibles in this book.

Table of Contents

About the Author

Ambrose "Broz" Panico is a veteran educator and change agent who has worked as a teacher, coach, dean, principal, State Due Process Hearing Officer, and central office administrator. Ambrose began his career as a teacher in a Chicago public school behavior disorders classroom and is currently the assistant director of the Exceptional Children Have Opportunities (ECHO) Joint Agreement, located in South Holland, Illinois. He has developed therapeutic public school options for students who require higher levels of support in order to succeed. Ambrose helps districts meet their students' needs in general education classrooms or district special programs. He also works with district personnel to create environments that enhance and support students who are attempting to behave better and to develop and implement behavior intervention plans that empower them to do so.

As a consultant, he has supported the efforts of like-minded educators on a national level. In addition to his public school career, he is a private professional development specialist, consultant, and trainer. His books, *Adventure Education for the Classroom Community: Over 90 Activities for Developing Character, Responsibility, and the Courage to Achieve* (2000) and *Discipline and the Classroom Community: Recapturing Control of Our Schools* (1999), and articles, "The Classroom Community Model: Teaching Responsibility" (1997) and "Service Learning as a Community Initiation" (1998), are evidence of his professional commitment to responsibility education.

Foreword

I worked in the Thornton School District 205 schools with Ambrose Panico many years ago, developing plans to improve student behavior and training teachers under his supervision using the principles and strategies of *Discipline With Dignity®*. His new book, *Behave Yourself!*, personifies the competent, caring, and professional nature that Ambrose brought to those trainings. A program can't work if it is too simplistic, leaves out the needs and concerns of the student, or relies predominantly on rewards and punishments. The strategies, questionnaires, and tools described in this book are not only relevant to the concerns of special education teachers, but to teachers of any disruptive student in any class or grade.

Student behavior does not exist in a vacuum. The context of the behavior is crucial in understanding its underlying cause, and in finding the keys to changing those behaviors that hurt the student's chances for success. More often than not, discovering the contextual clues makes sense of seemingly nonsensical behavior. We often wonder why a student does something that appears irrational and self-destructive, only to find later that it makes perfect sense to the student (who perceives the variables of context differently than we initially did).

Often students do the *right* thing in the *wrong* way. Fighting is a good example. It is natural and acceptable to defend oneself from verbal attack. Every student has the right to protect his or her own dignity. Fighting, however, is not the preferable way to do it. It is good to listen to a friend who might be upset or elated over something that just happened; however, doing so during class time is not the right time or place to do so. For an intervention to be successful, it must take into account the difference between *what* and *how*.

Another major concern that is addressed in this book is the issue of control. Many students have difficulties with control and seek to find it by proving that no one can make them do what they don't want to do. The truth is we cannot make students do anything unless they want to do it. All interventions that give students choices and acknowledge their power have a better chance of success than interventions that use power against them to force them to change in ways that they don't want to. The great power of this book is that it recognizes the need to give students control over the changes we believe are in their best interest. Using force simply will not work with our most difficult students. If it did, we would not have difficult students to begin with!

Another important distinction between typical books on behavior change and this book—especially for special education students—is the understanding of the limited use of rewards and punishments in the change process. Punishments and rewards satiate, meaning that more is needed to get the same effect. The first time a student is given a detention or a call is made to his parents, he will plead for mercy. After the third or fourth time he will say, "Who cares?!" As punishments satiate, we need stronger and more painful ones until there is no more pain we can inflict. It is far superior to teach students the skills and strategies they need to make better decisions than to punish the previous poor decisions made in the past.

Rewards also satiate. We start by giving something small, and soon find that students want more. "Is that all?" is a whine we have all heard many times. In addition, rewards used as bribes rather than appreciation can become addictive, and students will not learn without them. This book offers a far more holistic approach than simply rewarding good behavior and punishing the bad.

The best thing about this book is that it is comprehensive in its fundamental approach. It does not rely on any one philosophy or set of tools, but rather incorporates several sound methodologies, all of which are child-centered. The needs and goals of the student are paramount. Helping out a teacher might or might not help a child, but helping a child improve his or her behavior *always* helps a teacher. I agree with Ambrose's wonderful new book; we are always better off starting with the student.

—Dr. Richard L. Curwin
Coauthor of the *Discipline With Dignity* series

Preface

Start with the end in mind.

—*Stephen Covey*

I have worked as a professional development provider and a classroom consultant for over 30 years. The majority of my work has been helping teachers build caring classroom communities that encourage students to behave better, work harder, and reach their fullest potential. Whether I am providing classroom management strategies, techniques to limit disruptive behavior and avoid power struggles, or a process for developing individual student behavior change plans, my focus is on student empowerment. My message to teachers is to work smarter, not harder; position your students to control themselves so you don't have to—so you can teach. My work has afforded me a wonderful opportunity to keep learning in classroom "laboratories"; I have been very fortunate to work with committed teachers who were always willing to dialogue and offer feedback.

This book is the direct result of that work and an ongoing cycle of creating, implementing, debriefing, and refining the strategies, methods, and processes I offer my professional development participants. For many years now, I have been asking the same question of competent, caring teachers from all parts of the country and from both general and special education classrooms. That question is, "How do you change student behavior?" Their responses have given me the final push to finally put pen to paper: Most say that you change student behavior through some form of reward or punishment.

This strategy is almost exclusively based on behavior modification principles, and while it may be labeled *operant conditioning* or *reinforcement-based intervention,* it all reduces to the same thing: "If you do what I want, I will give you something." These are the same teachers who devise creative, engaging lessons and who become even more creative when a child fails to grasp an academic concept or skill. If a child fails to grasp an academic concept or skill, these teachers devise a way to reteach the concept or skill differently. They begin by carefully analyzing what they are asking the child to understand or to do and determining if the child possesses the necessary prerequisite understanding or skills. They do not routinely decide the child is simply refusing to learn or opting to fail. They make sure to consider the child's individual learning style with an eye toward tapping areas of strength, instead of stressing areas of relative weakness. They use the acumen the child brings to the new learning and build relevancy by pointing out real-world application possibilities.

It is hard for me to understand how competent, caring teachers could demonstrate their professional competency and sincere concern when designing and implementing academic instruction, *and* be so limited when designing strategies to help their students change their behavior. When asked to design plans to facilitate their students' discarding of undesirable maladaptive behaviors in favor of desirable adaptive behaviors, they are not nearly as creative.

I have a second reason for writing this book: my frustration with the quality of individual behavior intervention plans (BIPs) developed for special education students. Disturbingly, rather than engaging me in professional conversation regarding how we might really help our students change their behavior, too many of my special education colleagues choose to quiz me on how to stay in compliance with special education rules and regulations pertaining to the requirements for BIPs—in other words, how to stay out of "special education jail."

This book is not written with a focus on special education compliance issues; its focus is on issues of quality as they pertain to the development of sound behavior change plans for both general and special education students. It offers both general education and special education teachers new ways to think about helping their students change their behavior, strategies for developing BIPs that actually change student behavior, and the tools required to do so.

This process may be used as a foundation for ensuring that individual BIPs developed for special education students are viable, as required by the Individuals with Disabilities Education Improvement Act of 2004. While the Plan to Do Better forms were not designed to document compliance with local, state, and federal rules, the process does position you, the reader, to make individual student decisions that lead to the development of viable BIPs and compliance with not only the letter, but the intent of the law.

The Plan to Do Better forms are best suited for use with general education students and special education students whose individualized education program (IEP) team has determined they could benefit from individualized behavior intervention prior to (or instead of) formal BIP development.

IEP teams developing formal BIPs and using forms designed to document compliance are encouraged to use the Plan to Do Better essential questions listed in chapter 6 to secure student input, establish the function of the problem behavior, and select the behavior change tools listed in chapter 4; by doing so, the team makes certain to addresses issues of both regulation compliance and plan viability.

The Individuals with Disabilities Education Act (IDEA) of 1997 set in motion fundamental, conceptual, and practice changes in special education. As a result, special education became "a set of services, not a place. The law now required LEAs to develop educational services intended to address educational needs before children were labeled as disabled" (Batsche, Elliott, Graden, Grimes, Kovaleski, Prasse, Reschly, Schrag, & Tilly, 2005, p. 15).

This is not a special education manual. In fact, I hope this resource will blur the territorial lines often associated with general and special education—to help any educator work with any student to improve the student's behavior, regardless of the setting. IDEIA 2004 provides both support and motivation to do just that; to think in terms of one unified educational system as opposed to general education and special education operating parallel to one another. Nowhere is this made clearer than in the mandate for response to intervention (RTI):

> RTI is many things to many people. To some, RTI is an effort to promote the use of evidence-based instruction in classrooms; to others its goal is to make general, remedial, and special education work together in a more integrated way; and to still others, it is a means of identifying students as needing special education services, especially services for students who have learning disabilities (Division for Learning Disabilities, 2007).

To me, RTI is a practical problem-solving approach to providing meaningful intervention. RTI is often mistakenly viewed as addressing only academic problems; RTI is intended to address both academic and behavioral problems. It acknowledges the futility of attempting to separate out academic and behavioral challenges a child may present. Whether unmet academic challenges have resulted in problematic behavior or problematic behavior has resulted in a failure to benefit from instruction, RTI teams are charged with the responsibility to address both. Many RTI teams incorporate Positive Behavioral Interventions and Supports (PBIS), a problem-solving approach to addressing challenging behaviors, into their standard operating procedures. This is easily done as both RTI and PBIS offer interventions at three specific levels. Tier 1 consists of core interventions for all students in all settings. Tier 2 contains targeted group interventions for students at risk, and Tier 3 consists of intensive individual interventions for students experiencing serious difficulty.

Plan to Do Better provides RTI teams—and any team charged with the responsibility of developing Tier 3 interventions—very potent tools for doing so. Since Plan to Do Better is also a problem-solving process, it follows the same logical progression as RTI and PBIS. Teams welcome the Plan to Do Better process because they intuitively understand that it does not represent one more thing to put on their plate; it offers a means to clear their plate. In other words, it allows them to do what they are currently doing and achieve better outcomes for their students. The Plan to Do Better forms and process are very useful and easily incorporated into the work of RTI teams. These teams may either choose to use the Plan to Do Better forms and process in its entirety, or to selectively choose elements of the model to incorporate in their existing model. Many teams report good results by simply incorporating the plan's core beliefs, essential questions, and of course the behavior change tools into their existing process.

Chapter Overview

Chapter 1 explains why we may believe we either can't or shouldn't play a role in changing student behavior. Chapter 2 provides a theoretical perspective on human behavior from which to view your students, analyze the behavioral challenges they present, and think about changing behavior. This perspective lays the foundation for creating viable behavior change plans. Chapter 3 outlines the core beliefs behind best-practice interventions that should guide a team in developing individualized plans.

Chapter 4 then presents five tools for changing behavior, and chapter 5 describes a five-step problem-solving approach and provides a list of essential questions to answer during the process of creating a Plan to Do Better. Together, the tools and process allow theory to be put into practice.

Chapter 6 compiles resources—interviews, surveys, questionnaires, inventories, and profiles—useful in securing student, parental, and school personnel input on the behavior to be changed. And finally, chapter 7 shows sample behavior change plans created using the Plan to Do Better process and tools. These sample plans, supported with student profiles and narratives on student background, demonstrate how to use the tools in this book to address specific problem behavior for individual students. They may be used as a training aide for individuals or teams seeking to improve their skills in writing behavior change plans.

In closing, I offer this advice to readers who want to change student behaviors: Never do anything to your students that you would not want done to you. Never do anything for your students that they can do for themselves. Empower your students to do the things they think they cannot do.

Chapter 1

Why We Are Stuck on Rewards and Punishments

The farther backward you can look the farther forward you are likely to see.

—Winston Churchill

Teachers tend to limit themselves to using rewards and punishments to help students change their behavior. There are a few reasons for these self-imposed limitations, each with its own rationale.

Roles and Responsibilities

Some teachers believe it is not their job to teach their students to behave. They believe that they teach academic content and that *parents* teach appropriate behavior. They see their role in relationship to student behavior as limited to rewarding good behavior and punishing bad behavior so that academic instruction may occur uninterrupted. My response to these teachers is that they are dead wrong. If they do not examine their beliefs about student behavior, they will never accept the responsibility they have to their students (and to society) to actively participate with their students' parents to mold competent individuals and responsible citizens. You know your job is much more than teaching the ABCs and the 123s, or you would never have purchased this book.

Talk with your colleagues, lend them this book, and ask them to help you change a student's behavior—not because they must but because it is the right thing to do—and because the child needs them to do it; to appeal to them on a moral level. If they fail to be motivated by moral obligation, inspire them by suggesting there could be a link between academic instruction and problem behavior. Researchers have confirmed that students will misbehave to avoid the embarrassment associated with repeated failure (Dunlap, 1993; Nelson, Scott, & Polsgrove, 1999; Shores & Wehby, 1999).

Time Constraints

Some teachers simply resort to rewards and punishments because they are overwhelmed by competing demands on their time. Their principal refers to their multitude of pressing duties as *multitasking*, but that doesn't make the job any easier. These teachers believe they must spend all their time on academic instruction to survive in the era of No Child Left Behind, so discipline must be quick and easy (such as reward and punishment). They thoughtfully teach academic content, and they reactively levy discipline. But when discipline is reduced to a reactive endeavor based solely on rewards and punishments, it is ineffective for the 5 to 15% of students who desperately need a teacher's help to change their behavior. The word *discipline* is derived from the Latin *disciplina*, which refers to learning. For students requiring behavior change, discipline must be associated with more than rewards and punishments. They must come to view discipline as a collaborative process with their teachers that allows them to gain control of individual situations and their lives in general.

In fact, if you do not proactively engage your most challenging students in controlling their own behavior, you choose to attempt to control their behavior for them—over and over, after things have already gone wrong. Teachers who fail to understand this concept waste an excessive amount of time attempting to limit the disruptive behavior of a handful of students. Conversely, teachers who invest a relatively small amount of time in proactively helping these students change their behavior recoup a significant amount of instructional time that is not diverted to reactive discipline. At its core, this book is a practical "how to" resource for individuals who make the decision to proactively teach discipline.

Compliance Mindset

Special education's focus on compliance issues and students with developmental disabilities is impeding its ability to help higher functioning students change their behavior. Both general education and special education educators alike are confused by and often intimidated by special education's emphasis on rules and regulations as they pertain to helping students with disabilities change their behavior.

The reauthorization of the Individuals with Disabilities Education Improvement Act (IDEIA 2004) has in some ways only added to the confusion and heightened anxiety levels among educators by:

- ⚝ Mandating functional behavioral assessment (FBA) as part of a student's behavior intervention plan (BIP)
- ⚝ Failing to adequately define FBA or provide enough detail regarding its implementation

⁊ Linking the FBA/BIP procedure to the discipline process: "According to the IDEA 1997, schools must introduce functional behavioral assessment to address serious and persistent problem behavior" (Gable, Hendrickson, & Smith, 1999, p. 167). IDEIA 2004 continues to enforce this requirement for FBA and BIP.

When a child with a disability exhibits behavior that impedes the child's education or the education of the child's classmates, the use of positive behavioral interventions and supports must be considered. IDEA 1997 goes on to ensure that for disciplinary action that would result in a change of placement exceeding 10 consecutive school days, the child receives both appropriate functional behavioral assessment and behavioral intervention services intended to alleviate the recurrence of the objectionable behavior. Mitchell Yell (1997) is among many researchers and scholars who take the position that this requirement is applicable to all students with disabilities, regardless of their disability category.

While the law does not provide a specific definition of functional behavioral assessment, its clear intention is to ensure that the function or purpose of the behavior is not only identified, but also used to create a behavior intervention plan that teaches and encourages alternative behaviors that serve the same function as the undesirable behavior (Gable & Hendrickson, 2000). It should be of no surprise, in light of the emphasis of No Child Left Behind, that IDEIA 2004 [300–324 (3) (i)] mandates the "participation of a regular (general) education teacher in the determination of appropriate positive behavioral interventions and supports and other strategies for the child."

This is probably a good time to provide a definition of functional assessment for a general education teacher who wonders, "What else am I supposed to know and do?"

What Is a Functional Behavioral Assessment?

Sugai, Horner, and Sprague (1999, p. 253) define *functional assessment* as "the process of identifying establishing operations, antecedent variables, and consequent events that control target behaviors. Said differently, a functional assessment identifies when, where, and why problem behaviors occur and when, where, and why they do not occur." Individual states, districts, and schools are presently engaged in a struggle to figure out which students require functional behavioral assessment, which students would benefit from FBA, what constitutes FBA, who can and should conduct FBA, what to do with an assessment once you have it, and how to find the human and financial resources required to actually administer an FBA, and then to use the FBA findings to develop and implement the BIP. Yell notes that among other concerns, in passing the IDEA 1997 amendments, Congress found that "too much emphasis placed on procedural paperwork tied to legal requirements and not focused on teaching and learning, and better student outcomes, had limited the effectiveness of the IDEA" (IDEA 1997, p. 1). Unfortunately, the 2004 reauthorization of IDEA does not address this concern.

In other words, the emphasis placed on FBA might unintentionally perpetuate paperwork designed to ensure compliance with regulation at the expense of actually helping students change their behavior. Too often the focus becomes avoiding due process hearings and litigation instead of improving student outcomes. The result is often what I refer to as a *complete* BIP; that is, a plan with all the blanks filled in—a plan that is ready to be filed away because no one expects it to actually do anything to help a student change his or her behavior. Instead, the plan was meant only to keep everyone out of "special education jail." Compare that to a Plan to Do Better, which I refer to as a *viable* plan—a plan that each team member wants a copy of because everyone believes that if it is implemented with fidelity, there is a good chance the student will change his or her behavior.

Complete plans are written as if behavior occurs in a vacuum and pay little attention to the social, academic, and environmental variables that make up the context in which the behavior occurs. These plans often identify one nonproductive behavior and one intervention designed to address that behavior. These plans almost always overemphasize the use of punishments and rewards. In reality, many students present a myriad of problems that respond better to a bundling of interventions. This bundling "may need to include: behavioral-reduction, cognitive, and skill building programs, along with environmental manipulations" (Gable, Henrickson, Tonelson, & Van Acker, 2002, p. 469).

Finally, complete plans often totally disregard the importance of personal (internal) variables and instead focus entirely on environmental (external) variables. Viable plans, in contrast, recognize the need to balance a behavioral change equation that thoughtfully includes both personal and environmental variables. We are cautioned that "in all, a mix of variables affect student behavior encompassing internal and external events" (Gable, Hendrickson, Tonelson, & Van Acker, 2002, p. 463).

While federal regulations mandate the administration of FBA for all special education students who require BIPs, IDEIA 2004 does not require that direct observation be part of the assessment. Direct observation is the practice of one or more individuals observing the student to collect data regarding the antecedent events, the nonproductive problematic behavior, and the consequent events that control the behavior.

A review of the FBA literature reveals that most of the research that informs the use of FBA in the schools was conducted on individuals with low-incidence disabilities and extremely limited communication skills. These individuals were of limited cognitive ability (for example, individuals with severe and profound mental retardation). Gable, Hendrickson, and Smith (1999) not only support my assertion that most research has focused on low-incidence disabilities, they add a concern that few studies have focused on the effectiveness of FBAs with older children or students with average IQ scores.

Educators across the county are suffering from paralysis by analysis when it comes to developing BIPs for students of average or better cognitive ability—students who communicate verbally and whose troublesome behavior certainly does not qualify as aberrant. Traditional functional behavioral assessment that includes direct observation should not be standard operating procedure for all special education students experiencing challenging behaviors. Sugai, Horner, and Sprague (1999, p. 253) state:

The central issue for the articles in this issue of behavioral disorders is whether [FBA] procedures are important for the design of behavioral interventions. Our position is that a tremendous amount of preventative work and interventions for simple behavior problems can be accomplished without the time and expense required to conduct an [FBA]. However, when children do not respond to these simple efforts or when the behavior under concern is of a severe, violent, or intense nature, the use of [FBA] procedures is warranted.

Other researchers concur, questioning the wisdom of FBA for students who are not developmentally delayed and instead encouraging a judicious application of formal FBA. Nelson (1998) suggests that only about 1 to 3% of students evidencing chronic and intense misconduct require formal FBA, and 7 to 9% of students at high risk may be candidates for less elaborate efforts. Other researchers express concern that the methodology and instruments currently available may not be appropriate for higher functioning students in applied settings (Quinn, Gable, Fox, Rutherford, Van Acker, & Conroy, 2001).

Once practitioners decide for which students a formal FBA is appropriate, they must then wrestle with the logistics of actually conducting one. In their review of public policy as it relates to FBA in the schools, Howell and Nelson (1999) summarize the concerns of several researchers who characterize FBA as labor-intensive, taxing on resources and expertise, and frankly, mind-boggling! They conclude that the lack of practicality may limit widespread implementation. The challenging logistics go beyond the allocation of human resources and time. The need for direct observation, along with the need for individual data collection for higher functioning students, are sidetracked by the lack of appropriate research and validation of direct observation methods. As Quinn, Gable, Fox, Rutherford, Van Acker, and Conroy (2001, p. 262) note:

> Unfortunately, the majority of instruments that appear to be important to the FBA process, including various interview schedules or direct observation schema, have received little or no evaluation as to their reliability or validity. Furthermore, evaluation of instrument technical adequacy has been conducted largely within populations with developmental disabilities, which does not answer questions about their applicability to other populations.

In summary, when working with students of average or better intelligence whose behavior is not aberrant, it is advisable to first use the Plan to Do Better process to discern the function of the nonproductive behavior. If the team can do so with a reasonable degree of certainty, recommit human resources typically assigned to direct observation to viable plan development. Obviously, if the team cannot discern the function of the behavior, direct observation is indicated and should be conducted.

Who Is Qualified to Perform an FBA?

While there does not appear to be a specific certification or credential an individual must hold in order to conduct an FBA in a school setting, I agree with other researchers and writers in the field (Conroy, Clark, Gable, & Fox, 1999): There is an expectation that individuals be trained and competent in the application of FBA methods and instruments. The complex nature of many of the FBA processes and instruments can be daunting to school personnel even after training has been provided. In addressing the application of FBA for students with emotional and behavioral disabilities (EBD), Hendrickson, Gable, Conroy, Fox, and Smith (1999, p. 281) conclude, "Given that the research base of FBA techniques with students with EBD is in its early stage of development, it is no wonder that a majority of school districts' personnel lack the specific competencies and expertise to implement FBA." Van Acker, Boreson, Gable, and Potterton (2005, p. 37) only confirm what most practitioners know, that "there is a dearth of trained personnel available to conduct the functional assessments of behavior and to develop and implement the behavior intervention plans."

My own experience has left me saddened by the number of complete BIPs I encounter. The behavior intervention plans that I have the occasion to review routinely demonstrate no connection between the behavior's function and the implementation strategy. Just as disheartening is the fact that many rely solely on the use of rewards and punishments, too often tipping the scale in the direction of punishment. While I have noticed a trend to include proactive teaching of deficit skills and more productive behaviors, this trend is certainly not widespread. A review of the literature has done little to alleviate my concern. In a summary of their review of BIPs, Van Acker, Boreson, Gable, and Potterton (2005, p. 52) state:

> An alarming finding was the general disregard for the information gained in the FBA process when teams began to develop the behavior intervention plan. In almost 2/3 of the cases, there was little or no indication that the teams used information related to the function served by the behavior in their design of the BIP. Often teams simply continued to recommend the intervention plan previously used (despite its being ineffective). A number of the plans actually recommended the use of an intervention designed to reduce a problem behavior by providing a consequence similar in function to the target behavior. For example, one school recommended the use of suspension (which allows a child to avoid school) as a consequence for skipping school for a student with emotional and behavioral disorders (a student with high levels of anxiety and panic attacks who wanted to escape or avoid the classroom setting).

> Slightly more than half of the BIPs developed indicated the clear use of positive behavioral supports. There was a continued reliance on punishment procedures and many of the BIPs only indicted a proposed use of aversive procedures. There seems to be reluctance to employ, or a general unfamiliarity with the use of, positive approaches to behavior change.

Choose to engage your students, their parents, and your colleagues in developing and implementing viable behavior intervention plans—Plans to Do Better. Do not allow yourself to become mired in the controversy over IDEA and its requirement for functional behavioral assessment; think of FBA as a work in progress.

Moving Beyond Rewards and Punishments

The Plan to Do Better approach is a simple and direct five-step process for developing an individual behavior change plan for a student. It stresses student involvement in the process, and it is designed to yield at least as much information about the student as it does about the student's challenging behavior. By doing so, it fosters the development of a healthy relationship between the student, the student's parents, and school personnel. This relationship is often the foundation upon which the best plans are built. Plan to Do Better is predicated on the all-important notion that in order to help a student change his or her behavior, we must understand the connection between the behavior and the behavior's function. Then and only then can we develop a meaningful behavior change plan. Toward this end, the Plan to Do Better process outlined in this book provides five behavior change tools, detailed instructions, and specific practices.

Involve the students and their parents in the process, always consider the five tools, use as many as necessary to develop meaningful plans, and good things will happen. Recently I sat with a team to assess the effectiveness of a plan we had helped a first-year general education teacher develop for a very challenging second grader. The child's mother, a loving but stressed single parent, could be described as just as challenging. In the past, she had a habit of blaming everything on the teacher and questioning the teacher's competency. The teacher's smile and excited demeanor were all I had to see to know that good things were happening. The teacher gave a thorough report that not only confirmed changes in the child's behavior, but in the mother's as well. The teacher could not understand how this woman who had once targeted her had become her biggest supporter. I simply pushed the Plan to Do Better across the table and asked, "Wouldn't you support someone who did all this for your child?"

The teacher understood and smiled. She had provided the mother and the student the opportunity to be an integral part of the process, and together with the team, they developed a plan that went way past rewards and punishments; in fact, it included four of the five behavior change tools. The child felt better about herself, her teacher, and her prospects. The mother and the teacher were now partners; no one was attempting to fix blame—everyone was too busy finding solutions.

Things to Remember

⅏ The Plan to Do Better process is primarily intended for use with students who have average or better cognitive ability and whose method of communication is the spoken word. Remember, most of the research regarding functional behavioral assessment was conducted on individuals with severe developmental disabilities: individuals who were for the most part nonverbal.

⅏ Realize that formal FBA (which includes direct observation) may not be the preferred or necessary method of establishing the important connection between behavior and the function of the behavior, especially if you are working with higher functioning students. Make individual decisions for individual students regarding what constitutes functional behavioral assessment. Do not assume FBA always means laborious direct observation.

⅏ Do not allow yourself to be intimidated by self-proclaimed FBA experts. Many suffer from a myopic view of behavior as a result of their training and their work with populations with severe disabilities. When working with higher functioning individuals, the collective common sense of the individuals who work and live with the student is invaluable.

⅏ View FBA not as a set of rigid procedures, but as a way of thinking about behavior and how to change it. Never underestimate the importance of knowing the function of the behavior. Make sure that this knowledge informs the development of the behavior intervention plan.

⅏ Before conducting a direct observation for all students in need of a behavior intervention plan, the intervention team should first attempt to establish the function of the undesirable behavior without the benefit of direct observation. If the team is unable to establish the behavior's function through the Plan to Do Better process, then and only then is direct observation required. Devote your team's time and energy to the development of a viable behavior intervention plan rather than unnecessary direct observation activities.

⅏ Always involve students in the development of their behavior intervention plans. Since you have the advantage of working with students who understand the spoken word, ask them why they engage in the nonproductive behavior— they just might tell you. Encourage them to help you design a plan to change their behavior. Their enthusiasm and insightfulness might surprise you.

⅏ Focus a little less on the specific problem behavior and a little more on your student. The Plan to Do Better process is designed to help you gain useful information about the *person*, which will help you address the behavior.

⅏ Focus a little less on the specific behavior, and a little more on your *relationship* with your students and their parents. The Plan to Do Better process is designed to support the relationship; often it is the relationship that allows the behavior intervention plan to be implemented and the student to succeed.

- Realize that although it is easiest to think of behavior change in terms of one specific behavior, the higher functioning the student is, the less productive this thinking is. Avoid the trap of thinking in a linear progression of antecedent-behavior-consequence. Teams who think in this simplistic fashion almost always end up designing plans based entirely on rewards and punishments.

- Make sure whatever your FBA and behavior intervention plan is, it accounts not only for environmental (external) variables, but also for personal (internal) variables.

- Be sure to design intervention plans that go beyond reward and punishment. Be sure to always consider the five behavior change tools. Remember that often it is necessary to bundle *several* behavior change tools together to effect significant change.

- Always work as problem-solving teams when designing behavior intervention plans.

There are those who would attempt to reduce the complicated art of helping a troubled child change behavior to bad science. At its core, this book is a reaction to those people. It is a declaration that life is more than stimulus-response—life is about understanding that we have the freedom and power to always choose our responses. Our mission is not to control our students. Our mission is to help them understand that they control themselves. Covey states, "Between stimulus and response, there lies a space. In that space lies our freedom and power to choose our response. In our response lies our growth and our happiness" (1997, p. 27). Covey goes on to explain that this freedom to choose is the foundation for four human gifts: self-awareness, conscience, imagination, and independent will. These are the understandings; these are the gifts we must give to our students if our behavior intervention is to have any real and lasting effect.

Chapter 2

A Practitioner's Guide to Understanding Human Behavior

The heart has its reasons which reason knows not of.

—*Blaise Pascal*

Some theorists, such as B. F. Skinner, John B. Watson, and Edward Thorndike, maintain that all behavior is a function of the interaction between the behavior and the environment. These theorists reject the notion that behavior is influenced and possibly controlled by theoretical constructs (such as the mind, the self, and the individual will). This definition of behavior (put forward primarily by behaviorists) is extremely limiting to teachers, school psychologists, school social workers, speech pathologists, and building principals who are working with students capable of communicating through speech.

The practitioner is much better informed by the definition of behavior offered by social cognitive theorists such as Albert Bandura. His theory of *reciprocal determinism* is extremely informative to a practitioner interested in a better understanding of how their students' behavior is formed and maintained (Bandura, 1974, 1977). In Bandura's understanding, human behavior is "the result of reciprocal influences between the personal variables (internal) of the individual, the environment (external) in which the behavior occurs, and the behavior itself" (Kaplan, 2000, p. 3). These internal, personal variables include:

- Cognitions (beliefs, expectations, values, perceptions, awareness, problem-solving)
- Emotions (anger, anxiety, depression)
- Competencies (social skills, self-management)
- Physical characteristics (attractiveness, race, size, social attributes) (Kaplan, 2000, p. 3)

External environmental variables, by contrast, include:

💯 Antecedents (modeling, setting events, cues)

💯 Consequences (positive and negative reinforcement punishment, extinction) (Kaplan, 2000, p. 3)

These internal and external variables interact to form and maintain human behavior. We are constantly engaged in processing information. Anyone who has spent any time in the classroom working with students knows that each individual experiences events (antecedents or consequences) in his or her own unique way. This is because the environmental event is processed through the child's unique set of personal, internal variables. In other words, unlike Skinner's white rats, we are observers as well as participants. Add to this awareness of self and the emotions of the moment, and it is easy to see that the formation and maintenance of human behavior is a wonderfully textured and dynamic phenomenon.

In general, antecedents are experienced and processed through the individual's unique set of personal variables. Behavior is the individual's response to the processed antecedents. The behavior interacts with and upon the environment, producing a consequence. The consequence is experienced and processed through the individual's personal variables. The perceived feedback of the consequence will strengthen, weaken, or maintain the behavior. Please see Figure 2-1 for an illustration of this cycle.

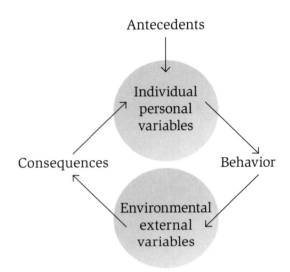

Figure 2-1: Behavior interacts with the environment to create consequences which strengthen or weaken it.

As a working practitioner and professional development provider, I have reviewed hundreds of functional behavioral assessments (FBAs) and their attendant behavior intervention plans (BIPs). Most FBAs give little attention to personal variables, and they rarely include perceived feedback (what the individual thinks happened) as part of the analysis. Instead, a narrow focus on environmental variables alone yields an FBA that often does not include sufficient information to develop a meaningful plan to help the individual change his or her behavior. Whether I am working with special educators engaged in a formal FBA and BIP, or with general education teachers struggling to figure out why their students behave the way they do (and how to help them change that behavior), I see a common denominator: the exclusion of valuable information.

Student Stories

Now let's look at two stories that illustrate the role personal and environmental variables play in the formation and maintenance of the behavior of two different students, Jeffrey and Bobby, in the same general education sixth-grade social studies class.

Jeffrey's Story

Personal Variables

Jeffrey believes he is not a competent student. He believes school is for the "smart kids." His parents do not value education, and he has adopted their view. His parents have been inconsistent in their attention to his needs, and he does not trust adults. He has never mastered even the most rudimentary anger management or problem-solving strategies and skills.

Environmental Event

The teacher, Mrs. Wise, gives Jeffrey his failing quiz paper and comments, "I'm sorry you didn't do too well. I hope you do better on our next quiz. Please let me know what I can do to help you."

Internal Processing of the Environmental Event and Initial Perceived Feedback

Jeffrey thinks to himself, "Same old, same old. I never do well in school. Why should I get this stuff? I didn't get the stuff from last year. Mrs. Wise doesn't really care about me or how I do."

Internal Emotional State

Jeffrey feels frustrated and angry, and has some feelings of abandonment. Overall, he feels hopeless.

Behavioral Output

Jeffrey tells Mrs. Wise, "This is baby stuff. Why do I need to learn it anyway? You're a stupid teacher." He crumples the quiz paper and throws it on the floor.

Environmental Response

Mrs. Wise tells Jeffrey to go to the dean's office and hands him a discipline referral.

Perceived Feedback

Jeffrey thinks, "Mrs. Wise really doesn't care. She's like all the rest. I'll never do well in school. There's nothing I can do. I'm where I belong in the dean's office."

Bobby's Story

Personal Variables

Bobby believes he is a reasonably competent student. He believes he is one of the smarter kids. His parents value education, and they have passed this value on to Bobby. His parents have been caring and consistent, and Bobby trusts adults. He has age-appropriate anger management and problem-solving strategies and skills.

Environmental Event

The teacher, Mrs. Wise, gives Bobby his failing quiz paper and comments, "I'm sorry you didn't do too well. I hope you do better on our next quiz. Please let me know what I can do to help you."

Internal Processing of the Environmental Event and Initial Perceived Feedback

Bobby thinks to himself, "I usually do pretty well on these quizzes. Last year was a breeze. I know Mrs. Wise wants me to do well."

Internal Emotional State

Bobby is somewhat upset and disappointed. He is motivated by a desire to know why he failed.

Behavioral Output

Bobby asks Mrs. Wise for help, saying, "I'm not sure why I did so badly." Together, Bobby and Mrs. Wise identify the following factors:

- Bobby is a basketball player, and the team was preparing for a big game, so they had long practices.
- Bobby forgot to take his textbook home.
- Bobby did not do a good job of completing the quiz study guide the class worked on the day before they took the quiz.

Environmental Response

Mrs. Wise commends Bobby for seeking help. They discuss time management issues and solutions. They agree that Mrs. Wise will review the next quiz study guide after Bobby completes it and will help him make any necessary corrections.

Perceived Feedback

Bobby thinks, "Mrs. Wise really cares about me and how I do. She understood my situation and helped me figure out how to pass the next quiz. I'm back in control."

The Teacher's Story

In these two stories, the teacher took the same actions, but with radically different results. Adopting Bandura's definition of human behavior would have positioned Mrs. Wise to better discover the purpose of Jeffrey's behavior. She might then have considered interventions designed to address both his external (environmental) variables and internal (personal) variables, instead of simply sending him to the dean's office. With the right tools, she could have created a better plan to change his behavior instead of punishing him.

The Plan to Do Better Tools

Armed with this social-cognitive view of behavior, the practitioner is now positioned to recognize the purpose of the behavior and select the appropriate tool(s) to change that behavior. These tools are discussed in more depth in chapter 4 (page 25).

Reinforcement-Based Tools

Reinforcement-based tools manipulate rewards and punishments.

Peter is a third grader in a special education cross-categorical program. Peter is identified as having a moderate emotional disability. He is having difficulty completing in-class assignments.

The Intervention

First, Peter, his teacher, and his parents meet to discuss the situation; they agree that the work is appropriate and the workload manageable, but Peter lacks the internal motivation to complete his work. Peter's teacher and parents help him to develop a reinforcement menu of things he is willing to work for, both in school and at home. Finally, they write a contingency contract, indicating that a successful day will be defined as any day in which Peter completes all assignments with a minimum of 85% accuracy, and a successful week will be considered any week in which Peter has a minimum of 4 successful days. Successful days will be reinforced on a daily basis, when Peter selects a reward from the school reinforcement menu, and successful weeks will be reinforced on Fridays, when he selects a reward from the home reinforcement menu. The contingency contract is signed by Peter, his teacher, and his parents.

Belief-Based Tools

Belief-based tools provide new information, new ways of looking at old information, or a broader context for evaluating information that positions the student to substitute empowering beliefs for disabling beliefs.

Joey is a sixth grader who happens to be the baby of the family. His three older sisters cater to his every whim and always make sure he gets what he wants. Because of this, Joey believes he is entitled to whatever he wants, whenever he wants it. He also believes he must always be the winner and feels justified in doing whatever it takes to come out on top. He is a gifted athlete, and he has a difficult time accepting defeat; he typically acts out negatively when he doesn't win.

The Intervention

Joey loves football; he loves to play it, watch it, and talk about it. The movie *Remember the Titans* is used as a discussion format by the team to explore the concepts of fairness, teamwork, friendship, and winning and losing gracefully. Joey's disabling beliefs are being maintained by nonproductive self-talk. Joey is helped to substitute rational statements for irrational statements (for example, "I hate it when I don't win" is replaced with "I really like to win but so do the other guys. . . . I can handle it"). Joey selects six classmates to rate him on a sportsmanship inventory, and the responses are shared with Joey privately.

Skill-Based Tools

Skill-based tools teach a skill or skill set the student must master in order to be successful.

Mary is a third grader who believes she is supposed to control her anger. However, she reports that while she *wants* to control her anger, she just doesn't know how.

The Intervention

Mary is helped to identify her personal anger triggers. She is then taught the simple but effective skill of backward counting from 10 to 1. Finally, Mary practices using her new skill in several role-playing situations she develops with her teacher.

Needs-Based Tools

Needs-based tools identify the basic need gratified by a maladaptive or socially unacceptable behavior. After the need is identified, an adaptive and socially acceptable behavior is substituted that meets the identified need.

Vennie is a 10th grader who does not have a positive male role model in his life. He lives in a community where gangs are common and older gang members are always looking for soldiers—boys who can be recruited to do their bidding. Vennie's need to belong is met by his membership in a street gang. He very much enjoys the attention his gang activity earns him from senior gang members.

The Intervention

First, Vennie is helped by the team to identify the very basic need that his gang membership fills. Then he is helped to identify activities that might meet his need to belong but won't put him or anyone else in jeopardy. He is enrolled in a mentor program that pairs protégés and mentors based on common interests. Vennie and his mentor share a love for automotive technology. His mentor has much to teach Vennie, all within the context of a healthy relationship. Vennie also finds belonging in the form of membership in the car club his mentor belongs to; this exposes him to several more positive male role models.

Environment-Based Tools

Environment-based tools seek to change behavior through thoughtful adaptations to environmental variables (such as physical setting, seat assignments, instructional level, presentation of instruction, assignment length, change of personnel, choice of academic class order, provision of a verbal cue to initiate a replacement behavior, or provision of an in-class control center).

Jatodd is a ninth grader who is experiencing difficulty mastering basic algebra concepts. He is embarrassed by the manner in which his math teacher provides correction, and he has been acting out in response to this correction.

The Intervention

Jatodd is asked, "What do you think could be done to help you perform better in math?" He suggests that he might do better with another teacher, and he requests to have his math class changed to earlier in the day. He offers that he has a hard time staying awake when he currently has math, right after lunch. Jatodd's math class is changed to first hour, his new teacher is willing and able to work with Jatodd, and he engages Jatodd in a discussion to find out how he can meet Jatodd's educational needs. His new teacher also assures Jatodd that he will not be put on the spot and agrees to only call on Jatodd when he raises his hand with a closed fist (indicating that he is sure about his answer). Finally, the teacher secures a commitment from Jatodd that he will participate in a tutorial math session he runs during Jatodd's study hall period.

All of these tools, combined with the 10 core beliefs identified in the next chapter, are vital to the success of behavioral change processes. The beliefs provide basic assumptions about changing behavior intended to guide the team's decision-making process. The tools offer specific intervention strategies for the team's consideration and prescriptive selection.

Chapter 3

Core Beliefs to Guide Implementation

The real act of discovery consists not in finding new lands but in seeing with new eyes.

—*Marcel Proust*

This chapter presents 10 beliefs or assumptions that are important to anyone engaged in helping a student change his or her behavior. Individuals and teams involved in the process of developing behavior change plans are encouraged to review these beliefs periodically. Doing so will help ensure the quality of the plans and the student's potential for success.

Belief One: Human Behavior Is Complex

Human behavior is a complex phenomenon that cannot be adequately explained by behaviorist theory, as we have seen in chapter 2. Instead, human behavior is best explained by constructs of social cognitive theory that describe a reciprocal relationship between environmental variables, personal variables, and the behavior itself. Human beings are both participants and observers to their own behavior. As such, perceived feedback is an important variable to consider when attempting to understand the function of a behavior, and ultimately when helping an individual change his or her behavior. For example, a student struggling to learn to control his anger may perceive himself and his plan as a failure because he has not been successful 100% of the time. The team points out to the student that he has been able to control his anger 100% of the time in three of five specific settings. After praising the student's effort, the team engages the student in designing plan adjustments for the remaining problem settings.

Belief Two: Misbehavior Is Not Always Willful

It is always a mistake to assume the student is being willfully disobedient—the behavior may not be under the student's control. Knowing if the behavior is under the student's control informs the behavior intervention. In fact, if the behavior is not under the student's control, the intervention may actually be an accommodation (for example, if the student is not developmentally ready to sit for the standard instructional period, the period could be shortened). In some cases, the behavior could be under the student's control if support is provided (for example, if the student is developmentally ready to sit for the standard instructional period when prompted by the teacher, the teacher can provide prompts every 10 minutes). However, if the student enjoys the behavior's consequence, the behavior is under the student's control (for example, if the student feels the teacher is unfair and plays favorites, the student may enjoy disrupting the teacher's instruction, in which case the motivation for the behavior and the student's perceptions must be addressed).

Belief Three: Long-Term Success Is the Goal

It is always best to start with the end in mind. Gable and Hendrickson (2000, p. 286) state, "Some current perspectives on FBA may be shortsighted and the IEP teams and other school personnel must look for ways to both deal immediately with impending behavior and promote long-term positive changes in student performance." While disruptive behavior patterns require specific intervention, the best intervention plans go beyond quick fixes to help students develop empowering beliefs and master fundamental skills on a long-term basis.

Empowering Student Beliefs

Empowering beliefs position a student to be successful in school and in life. Students who leave us with these empowering beliefs are prepared for whatever life brings. Examples of these beliefs are as follows:

Belief in personal competence—"I am competent. I can do it."

Belief in personal power and personal responsibility—"I accept that life is not always fair. However, I know that I significantly influence my outcomes."

Belief in the importance of significant relationships—"I am important to other people, and other people are important to me."

Belief in social contracts—"I have something to offer the community, and the community has something to offer me."

Fundamental Intrapersonal Skills

Fundamental intrapersonal skills allow students to make sense out of their world and to predict and control their outcomes. Such skills are:

- Ability to delay gratification
- Ability to predict outcomes
- Ability to learn from experience
- Ability to make reasonable decisions
- Ability to set goals
- Ability to work within the conventions and limitations of specific institutions and society at large
- Ability to respond to the frustrations of daily life in a flexible, resilient, and adaptive manner

Fundamental Interpersonal Skills

Fundamental interpersonal skills are prerequisites to success in all social settings—in school, at home, out in the community, and in the workplace. More than any other reason, a lack of interpersonal skills is cited as the cause of teenagers and young adults losing employment. Examples of these interpersonal skills include:

- Ability to work productively with individuals
- Ability to work productively in groups
- Mastery of basic communication, cooperation, negotiation, and conflict resolution skills

Belief Four: Teamwork Is Critical

The best intervention plans are usually developed by small teams of people working together. In putting quality functional behavioral assessment into practice in schools, a research agenda states on behalf of students with emotional or behavioral disabilities:

> With regard to both the legal requirements relating to student discipline and FBA and emergency standards of best practice within the field, there are a number of issues facing school personnel. These issues include (a) the need for a team-based approach to FBA and the behavior intervention plan (BIP); b) the requirement that general educators be a part of that team and to implement the BIP within the regular classroom; (c) the need to use multiple, different methods and sources of information to conducting the FBA and development of the BIP; (d) the need to have the FBA and BIP tailored to the particular needs of the student and his or her behavior; (e) the requirement that personnel be trained and be competent in the application of FBA methods and instruments; and (f) the need for schools to proactively address the behavioral needs of students with disabilities rather than simply waiting until they are legally required to deal with the behavior (Conroy, Clark, Gable, & Fox, 1999).

While surveys and narratives are useful data-gathering tools, nothing takes the place of brainstorming and dialogue. Besides, it is just more fun to work together. Usually the people who work with the student on a daily basis already have the information necessary to develop a meaningful behavior change plan. These individuals must come together to form a behavior change team so they may exchange, compare, contrast, and engage in dialogue. Never has the adage "two heads are better than one" been more applicable.

In preparation for the behavior change team meeting, individual members of the team conduct a review of the student's records, including academic performance, intellectual ability, and discipline history. Team members should be included based on their ability either to add relevant information or to analyze information. Review the questions provided in chapter 5 (page 39) to determine who to include. The team should include individuals who have observed the student both engaging in the problem behavior *and* behaving appropriately. Teams typically include the classroom teacher(s), personnel responsible for discipline, and personnel with knowledge of the behavior change process (such as a social worker or psychologist). Teams may also include others with knowledge of the specific nonproductive behavior (such as hall monitors, lunchroom or playground supervisors, and bus drivers) or the student's personal life (such as the student himself, parents, former teachers, coaches, church personnel, community mentors, and so on).

Belief Five: The Student Must Be Involved

The student must be viewed as an integral part of the solution, instead of the problem. Most practitioners indicate an understanding of the importance of student inclusion in the plan development process. However, researchers indicate that when interviews are used as an indirect data collection strategy, interviews with the student are only conducted 37% of the time (Van Acker et al., 2005). Our students are intelligent individuals, capable of sharing important information not only about the function of their behavior—and how personal and environmental variables are interfacing to maintain inappropriate behaviors—but also about how to craft a successful BIP to change that behavior. Securing the student's view is necessary for the plan's success. At what point and how this is done will depend on the student's age, intellect, and social-emotional maturity, and the team's personality (the term *personality* refers to whether the team is collectively authoritative or democratic, open- or close-minded, easily threatened or secure, and so on). The team may choose to secure the student's input prior to the team meeting without including the student at the meeting, may choose to secure the student's input prior to the team meeting and include the student at the meeting, may decide to have the student at the meeting to give input then, or any combination of those things.

Include the student as much as possible in every step of the plan's development. Nothing demonstrates respect and caring like including a student in the development of his or her own BIP. Doing so may initiate and maintain a sound student-adult relationship. This relationship may be what sustains a student when it gets tough to fulfill his or her part of a Plan to Do Better. As Van Acker (1998) notes, "The importance of our relationship with students, especially those most at risk for school failure and the display of challenging behavior cannot be stressed enough. In many cases, the strength of this relationship is what leads to improved behavior" (p. 3).

It is also important to view the student's parents, guardians, and caregivers in the same inclusive way. Even the most difficult families can be productive partners when they understand the goal: finding a solution instead of assigning the blame. Working with a student and their significant adults in this manner is also a wonderful way to build a trusting relationship, a relationship that will position school personnel to support the student and his or her significant adults to "stay the course" when the going gets tough. This relationship and buy-in to the process are often what make the difference between success and failure. It is never what we do *to* or *for* our students, but what we do *with* them that causes significant and lasting change.

Belief Six: Flexibility Is Critical

The team must be flexible in its development of behavior change plans. The team must be willing not only to think outside of the box, but also to build a *new* box. Every effort must be made to manipulate environmental variables in order to discourage inappropriate behavior and promote appropriate behavior. Accordingly, rather than only scrutinizing student behavior, the team must carefully analyze *adult* behavior as well to determine its influence. A good rule of thumb is to change adult behavior in order to change student behavior; it is silly to keep doing the same old thing and expect a different outcome. Adults should be willing to seek additional knowledge and master new skills deemed necessary to change behavior.

Belief Seven: Optimism Is Critical

The best plans are often demanding, but not impossible. They are also energizing because those who must implement them believe in their efficacy. I challenge team members to adopt a "whatever it takes" attitude. Teams are encouraged to brainstorm before evaluating, and not to rule an idea out just because that is not how it has been done in the past. Team members should regularly push themselves and their other team members to work outside their zone of comfort to help create and implement viable plans.

Belief Eight: Patience Is Critical

Behavioral change, especially change using belief-based interventions, takes time. It is a process, not a one-time event. Students took years to develop their beliefs; we must provide adequate time for them to evaluate these beliefs and, where necessary, change them. We must provide new information to challenge disabling beliefs and be sure to help the student process this new information.

Belief Nine: The Plan Must Be Positive

In *Positive Discipline in the Classroom*, the authors ask, "Where did we ever get the crazy idea that to make people do better, first we have to make them feel worse?" (Nelson, Lott, & Glenn, 1993, p. 79). It is futile to engage in an escalating process designed to make the student feel bad enough to try harder. Students do better when they feel *better* about themselves, their teacher, their classmates, and their prospects. The best plans make sure to reward productive behavior, especially if the plans are punishing nonproductive behavior. A plan may find it necessary to use some form of punishment to limit aggressive behavior; however, it must also include measures designed to maintain a positive teacher-to-student relationship (such as a post-punishment processing conference for the teacher and student).

Belief Ten: The Plan Must Go Beyond Reinforcement

The best plans go beyond reward and punishment. They thoughtfully and prescriptively select and apply not only reinforcement-based interventions, but also belief-based, skill-based, needs-based, and environment-based interventions. As Nelson et al. (1993) explain, "Teachers often choose a punishment/reward system because they believe that it teaches children responsibility. However, this system makes the teacher responsible, not the students. It is the teacher's responsibility to catch students being good and reward them, or catch them being bad and punish them. What happens when the teacher is not around?" (p. 9). Plans based on reward and punishment develop individuals who require external control; plans that go beyond reward and punishment develop individuals who exercise internal control.

Combine these beliefs with the behavior change tools in the next chapter, and your chances for a successful behavior intervention increase by leaps and bounds.

Chapter 4

The Five Behavior Change Tools

Far from disheartening your pupils' youthful courage, spare nothing to lift up their souls; make them your equals in order that they may become your equals.

—*Jean-Jacques Rousseau*

The Plan to Do Better process focuses the intervention team's effort on developing *viable* solutions for challenging behaviors. To that end, the team must consider not only the typical reinforcement-based interventions, but four other kinds of interventions as well: belief-based, skill-based, needs-based, and environment-based interventions. Teams will often incorporate several behavior change tools in the development of a single plan.

The need to go beyond the simple application of reinforcement-based behavior change tools is well-documented (see the work of Gable, Hendrickson, Tonelson, & Van Acker, 2002, on students with emotional and behavioral disabilities). *Belief-based tools* help us distinguish between behavior (skill) deficits and cognitive (belief) deficits, as Nichols (2001) has argued we must; students sometimes need instruction that challenges their long-standing cognitive distortions before they can change behaviors. *Skill-based tools* teach both interpersonal and (more recently) intrapersonal skills. Van Acker (1998) simply says that when a child has an interpersonal skill deficit, our logical course of action is to teach the skill. (He further notes that once the skill is taught, a reinforcement-based program may be required.) Olson and Platt (2000) offer various cognitive mediation strategies— such as self-talk, self-instruction, and self-evaluation—to develop intrapersonal skills and ultimate self-control of overt behavior. *Needs-based tools* are supported by the work of Glasser (1996), who pioneered the notion that needs drive behavior and that students may be provided alternative socially acceptable behaviors to meet their very legitimate needs. He stresses the need to "(1) survive and reproduce but also, (2) to belong and love, (3) to gain power, (4) to be free, and (5) to have fun" (Glasser, 2001, p. 25). Finally, it is accepted practice that the careful manipulation of environmental variables through *environment-based tools* may be necessary to support behavioral change (Gable et al., 2000).

By discussing these other kinds of tools, this chapter mediates against the over- and misuse of the most widely applied behavior change tool: reinforcement-based interventions. As we shall see, reinforcement-based tools have their uses, but they should never be the only option.

Reinforcement-Based Tools

Definition

Any intervention that seeks to change behavior through thoughtful manipulation of rewards and/or punishments

This form of intervention works entirely with the consequences of behavior. Some examples follow:

- ﹞ A student stays on task for 15 minutes and receives his teacher's praise.
- ﹞ A student stays on task for 30 minutes in order to receive a token; when she accumulates 12 tokens, she may choose an item from the school store.
- ﹞ A student is allowed to listen to music or play a video game after he completes his assignment.
- ﹞ A student who pushes and hits other students during structured play sits out for a designated period of time.
- ﹞ A student, her parent, and the teacher draft a contingency contract that stipulates that if she has a successful week (for example, no referrals to the office and all class and homework assignments completed with at least 80% proficiency), the student will be allowed to choose the Friday night family activity from a predetermined list of choices.

The law of reinforcement states that living organisms tend to repeat those behaviors that result in rewards or other desirable outcomes and tend to avoid those behaviors that fail to produce rewards or produce negative outcomes. In other words, any behavior that is followed by a reward or positive outcome is more likely to increase in frequency, and any behavior that is followed by a negative outcome is more likely to decrease in frequency (see Table 4-1). Behavior followed by the removal of a *negative* outcome or condition is likely to *increase*, and conversely, behavior followed by the removal of a *positive* outcome or condition is likely to *decrease*.

Table 4-1: Reward and Punishment Matrix

	Reward Increases Behavior	Punishment Decreases Behavior
Positive Reinforcement	When a positive stimulus (something that is desired) follows a behavior, the occurrence of that behavior is likely to increase (for example, a student completes his assignment and is given a favorite pencil).	When a negative stimulus follows a behavior, the frequency of the behavior is likely to decrease (for example, a student who fights is placed in an isolated time-out).
Negative Reinforcement	Removal of a negative stimulus after the occurrence of a behavior is likely to increase the frequency of the behavior (for example, a student's restriction on classroom privileges is removed once she completes and turns in her missing homework).	Removal of a positive stimulus after the occurrence of a behavior is likely to decrease the frequency of the behavior (for example, a student who takes other students' toys loses play time).

Unfortunately, reinforcement-based tools are often misused, and the problem is compounded by *degree-based thinking:* The teacher or team reasons that if the reward did not work, the problem isn't that they used the wrong tool, but rather that the reward was not big enough. A worse and possibly more common problem occurs when a punishment does not produce the desired effect and a more severe punishment is administered. Degree-based thinking doesn't ask whether the correct behavior change tool is being used; instead, it looks for sweeter M&Ms® and bigger hammers.

Things to Remember

Keep your focus positive. It is better to reward an incompatible behavior than it is to punish an undesirable behavior (that is, it is better, for example, to reward a student for staying in his seat than to punish out-of-seat behavior). Positive reinforcement builds and maintains the relationship between the teacher and the student; punishment can damage or destroy the relationship.

Be consistent. If you decide to punish the undesirable behavior, decide also to reward the incompatible behavior. This technique can mediate the negative effects of punishment.

Limit your use of punishment. Save punishment for serious behaviors and safety issues (for example, punish students to ensure the immediate cessation of physical aggression). The judicious use of punishment has several preferred outcomes: It preserves a caring classroom culture, preserves positive teacher-student relationships, and maintains its effect because it is not a regular occurrence.

Be sure you know what the student considers reinforcing. The easiest way to determine this is to ask. Remember:

- Reinforcements do not have to be tangible; use both tangible and intangible reinforcers. A tangible reinforcer might take the form of a sticker, a fancy pencil, or a trip to the movies; an intangible reinforcer might be praise or time spent with a favorite teacher.

- Strict behaviorists insist on moving from tangible to intangible reinforcers; experience tells us to use both.

- Even a favorite reinforcer can lose its potency, so use several options.

- Have your student work with you to create a reinforcement menu (see chapter 6, "Behavior Interview and Reinforcement Survey," page 59). This involvement is a great way to get the student to buy into the process, and develop planning and decision-making skills.

Start with the end in mind, and share that end with the student. If your goal is for the student to someday navigate life without a behavior intervention plan, it makes sense to let him or her in on it. Obviously the conversation must be guided by the student's age, intellect, and level of maturity. Even if you believe your student is too young, not that smart, and very immature—have the conversation anyway! Approaching the student in this manner does several things. First, it communicates that you consider your student an intelligent, thinking, responsible individual. Secondly, it communicates your expectation that the student will learn to manage his or her own behavior. Finally, it allows you to work *with* the student, not *on* the student.

Include the student in the assessment of whether or not reinforcements have been earned. Typical practice is to gradually move from teacher assessment, to teacher-student assessment, to student-teacher assessment, to student assessment. This is another way to avoid working *on* your student, and instead work *with* your student. It brings the student into the process and also shifts the locus of control from an external source (you) to an internal source (the student). Share with the student the awesome idea that the two of you have "an end in mind" and that you are working together to achieve it. You are not a police officer waiting to catch the student and write the ticket, and you're not Santa Claus hoping to find the student being nice instead of naughty so you may deliver the goods. You are a facilitator, a mentor willing to employ some temporary external structure while the student develops a personal, internal structure. The student needs to know this stuff—and can understand it.

Belief-Based Tools

Definition

Any intervention that seeks to change behavior by helping the student to examine and discard disabling beliefs in favor of empowering ones

This form of intervention provides experiences that facilitate the student's receipt of new information and new ways to perceive old information. It also provides a broader context for evaluating information and past, present, and future situations.

For instance, say that a student believes that in order to be a man, he must "take care of his business" and never allow himself to be "punked out." This student is provided with new information by spending 6 weeks reading the book *Makes Me Wanna Holler* (McCall, 1995) with a small group of his peers who share the same disabling belief. A social worker and teacher facilitate the group's discussion of how the main character's view of what a man is changes over the course of the book, and how his behavior changes to conform to his new belief.

Another student believes that only suckers and chumps work hard over an extended period of time to get the things they want. The student views the movie *A Bronx Tale* (DeNiro [Director/Producer], 1993) in a series of sessions with the school psychologist. The characters and the decisions they make provide new material for the student's consideration and for therapeutic discussion. The student also participates in the school's service-learning program that partners with Habitat for Humanity. An experience such as spending 6 months rehabilitating a dilapidated house allows the student to benefit from seeing and experiencing firsthand the effects of a group of people showing up every day and working hard side by side with the family that will eventually reside in a sound home.

Finally, consider a student who believes that his "bad temper" causes him to act out; his belief provides a built-in excuse for not accepting the resulting consequences. The student spends time talking with a teacher he admires and trusts. The teacher shares how and why he himself refuses to react violently when he is challenged, making sure to share not only his behaviors, but the beliefs (he controls his behavior and is responsible for the consequences of the behavior he chooses) that predispose him to behave the way he does. The teacher explains the short-term and long-term consequences for both himself and others, being sure to provide concrete examples (such as, "If I was to strike a student because he called me a name in front of the whole class, my students might fear me instead of trust me; I would lose my job, I could not support my family, and my wife and children might not think my temper was to blame—they might blame me").

Things to Remember

There are many ways to provide new information that challenges disabling beliefs. Some of those include:

- Readings, books, short stories, and magazine articles
- Feature films or videos, short subject films, and documentary films or videos
- Dialogue with an adult the student trusts
- One-on-one dialogue with a student who has made similar belief changes
- Participation in peer group discussion centered on belief change
- Presentation of evidence (for example, a student who does not value an education is shown the difference in earning power among a non–high school graduate, a high school graduate, and a college graduate)
- Real-life experiences (for example, a student who believes there is nothing to be gained by helping others participates in a service learning tutoring project)

Beliefs are difficult to impact and usually slow to change. Life-altering, dramatic events do happen and can cause immediate and significant belief changes, from "it can't happen to me" to "it can happen to anyone." For example, a student who lost a friend to the gang lifestyle might be motivated to leave the gang due to that loss. However, these unpredictable events are seldom involved with the behavior intervention plans we write. It is also important to realize that these events can often affect beliefs differently than hoped. For example, the student who lost the friend to the gang lifestyle might become even more reckless. In this case, the underlying belief changes from "it can't happen to me" to "it didn't and won't happen to me."

Most belief changes you will help your students make will be less dramatic and will not be the result of the impact of a single event, but rather the cumulative result of an ongoing series of events. For example, a student who believes she cannot master the academic content will require continued evidence (most likely in the form of assignments completed, quizzes and tests passed, and grades earned over an extended period of time) in order to alter her belief.

Belief changes require the student to make connections (connecting the dots). The belief change just described may also require the teacher linking the student's behavior to the desired outcome to show cause and effect: "You completed all assignments, you took your book home and reviewed the material nightly, you completed the test study guide, and you reviewed the study guide with your learning partner—and you passed the test. Congratulations!"

Beliefs are difficult to change; however, if you write a successful belief-based intervention plan, you do something of tremendous significance for your student. Because beliefs are an internal variable, the student carries them across time and space. In other words, beliefs will affect the student in all situations at all times, and more importantly, you will not be required to be there to prompt, to reinforce, or to punish.

Belief-based interventions cause the student to develop an internal locus of control. The student who comes to believe she is responsible for her own outcomes will benefit from her experiences, learn from them, and alter her behavior accordingly.

Behavior change is based on *belief* change; it does not occur the other way around. Students do not usually or easily behave in ways that are contrary to their beliefs. A student who believes she is entitled to always get what she wants will experience difficulty delaying gratification, even when she is reinforced for doing so. A student who believes he is a man only when he behaves in an aggressive manner will have difficulty behaving only assertively, even when assertive behavior is reinforced. A student who believes he is always supposed to win will bully classmates, even when bullying behavior is punished.

Conversely, change the belief, and the behavior will follow. A student who believes she is supposed to work hard to get what she wants will work hard and delay gratification. A student who believes he is a man when he resolves conflict in a peaceful manner will resolve his conflicts peacefully. And a student who understands life is about winning and losing will do both gracefully.

Belief change not only requires the use of belief-based interventions, but also the use of skill- and reinforcement-based interventions. A student who believes he is a man only when he meets any challenge by fighting must first be helped to alter his belief. Once the belief is corrected, he may need to develop a new set of skills for backing out of potential fight situations.

During the initial period of behavioral change, it is often productive to create a reinforcement-based intervention to encourage the student to use the new skills. The sequence of interventions is implemented as follows: belief-based intervention, then skill-based intervention, then reinforcement-based intervention. This is logical and fits our linear way of thinking. However, in the trenches of behavior intervention, you are encouraged to do what you think will work. It is not uncommon to implement all three interventions simultaneously.

Skill-Based Tools

Definition

Any intervention that seeks to change behavior by teaching the student a specific skill or skill set necessary for the student to succeed in engaging in a productive replacement behavior

Skill-based tools are necessary in the following kinds of situations:

- A student who disrupts group activities and angers other students through misguided attempts to be included is taught the social skill of "joining in"

    %% A student who wants to control her anger but has no socially acceptable way of doing so is taught the skills of backward counting and imagery

    %% A student who is never able to complete long-term assignments on time receives instruction in basic time management strategies

    %% A student who misbehaves during math class receives remedial instruction to allow her to be competent (for example, basic math skills required for meaningful class participation)

Skill-based interventions are used when the student wants to behave appropriately and be productive but simply does not posses the required skill set to do so. A student who never completes long-term assignments because she does not believe in the value of education requires a belief-based intervention, but a student who values education and never completes long-term assignments because she has no organizational or time-management skills requires a skill-based intervention.

Things to Remember

Students require a full repertoire of skills to be successful in school and in life. These skills, both intrapersonal and interpersonal, are presented in chapter 3 (page 21).

Students must possess the basic academic skills required for meaningful participation in the curriculum. Too often, intervention plans focus solely on behavior and social concerns and skills, and fail to address the underlying cause of the inappropriate behavior, which is sometimes a basic academic skill deficit. When indicated, behavior intervention plans must include academic skill-based interventions.

Consider the specific environment in which the behavior occurs (such as math class, physical education class, the playground, and so on), and task-analyze that environment to develop a list of the skills required to allow for success. Different environments require different skills. Does the student have the skill set required? Have you observed the student using a skill in another environment that he should be using in the problematic environment? In that case, the student has mastered the required skill but needs instruction in skill selection and application. For example, suppose you see a student appropriately and effectively respond to teasing in the classroom environment; later, however, the same student responds to teasing on the playground with aggressive behavior. This student may benefit from an adult helping him to apply the skill set used in the classroom to the playground setting.

Always consider factors of age, individual rate of development, and identified disability. Many students need specific instruction to master skills their classmates simply acquire. While most students learn to discern when a classmate is just playing with them and when a classmate is actually threatening them, some need direct instruction to do so.

Focus on a few significant behaviors. Often the intervention team identifies several behaviors and related skills that require intervention. Which to choose? A good rule is to select the one or two that offer the most "bang for the buck" (for example, "If she could only do this, I could avoid sending her to the office; our class can tolerate the rest"). Another strategy is to sit down with the student, lay out the situation, and then simply ask, "Where would you like to start?"

Skill instruction must be followed by skill practice. The intervention plan may need to include role-playing exercises and guided practice in which an adult or classmate helps the student apply the skill in simulated scenarios. Once the student has mastered the skill in simulated scenarios, the student is ready for plastic-practice. Plastic-practice is when the teacher presents an imagined situation that requires the student to use the newly mastered skill. The teacher does this at any time during the day without warning. The teacher may wish to prompt the student to use the skill in question. For example, a student who has difficulty accepting negative feedback can learn the skill of accepting negative feedback through practice. The teacher informs the student that at any time the teacher may present him with a pretend failed test (red ink and all). The teacher will cue the student, and together they will plastic-practice the skill.

Consider videotaping a student who is attempting to master a particular social skill, and then viewing the tape together. This procedure offers insight for both the student and the teacher. The teacher can facilitate the process by asking the student the following questions: "Did you follow the specific skill steps?" "Did you do them in the proper sequence? "Was your verbal and nonverbal communication saying the same thing?" "Do you think you did a good job? What do we need to work on?"

Consider teaching a skill identified as part of an individual student's intervention plan to the whole class. Often several students could benefit from this instruction. This strategy also helps create a culture that recognizes that we are supposed to be learning more than just reading, writing, and arithmetic; it creates a culture of tolerance and acceptance. The lesson also can serve as an entry into a much-needed class discussion. For example, after learning the skill of responding to teasing, students can discuss how teasing affects school culture.

Consider compiling the skills from all individual plans and teaching them to the whole class. At times a teacher is involved with developing and implementing individual intervention plans for several students. Again, many more students can usually benefit from the skill instruction.

Consider using literature and movies to help a student identify specific skills and their relevance. This has proved to be a very engaging and highly effective intervention. The nature of books and movies is to entertain; their entertainment value means you have instant student cooperation. The use of a medium seems to avoid (or at least reduce) some of the emotional interference that confronting issues on a more straightforward personal level can cause.

Consider purchasing published programs of social skill instruction. These programs are readily available and offer banks of task-analyzed social skills; often sample role-playing vignettes are included. *Skillstreaming the Elementary School Child* (McGinnis, Goldstein, Sprafkin, & Gershaw, 1984) and *Skillstreaming the Adolescent* (Goldstein, Sprafkin, Gershaw, & Klein, 1980) are two such resources.

Needs-Based Tools

Definition

Any intervention that seeks to change behavior by identifying a basic need (to belong, to be competent, to experience independence, and to have fun and relax), and then providing the student with a replacement behavior that allows the student to gratify the identified need in a socially acceptable manner

Needs-based interventions are used in the following kinds of situations:

- A student who is fulfilling his need to belong by becoming a member of a gang is helped to join a swim club, basketball team, or mentor program.

- A student who is fulfilling her need to have fun by constantly clowning in class is given 2 minutes in the morning and 2 minutes in the afternoon to make the class laugh.

- A high school student who is protecting his need to be competent by acting out prior to math instruction is provided a plan for addressing his math deficits. The plan includes changing his schedule to allow him to take math first hour, when he feels he is better able to learn, and transferring his study hall to a tutorial math session taught by his new math teacher.

By using needs-based interventions with a student, you are positioning the student to analyze his or her own behavior. After all, the first step in controlling behavior is understanding its purpose.

Things to Remember

Consider teaching the relationship between the behaviors people engage in and the needs those behaviors help to fulfill. Help the student to understand that at some level, all behavior is purposeful. Remember that it is usually easier to start by making the connection between specific behaviors and physiological needs, and then moving to the relationship between specific behaviors and psychological needs. For some suggestions, read *Discipline and the Classroom Community: Recapturing Control of Our Schools* (Panico, 1999).

Make sure the student understands that you will always support his desire to fulfill his needs. Explain that while you will support that desire, you may challenge the specific behavior he chooses to use to do so. Further explain that needs are almost always okay, but for a behavior to be acceptable, it must be adaptive and fair. *Adaptive* means there is a reasonable chance of actually meeting the need. *Fair* means the specific behavior is safe for self and others, and does not limit the right of others to meet their needs.

Some students will find it easy to identify the need the objectionable behavior is meant to meet, but most will require your assistance. It can be very useful to ask the student how she feels when engaged in the behavior. In attempting to find a replacement behavior that is both adaptive and fair, ask the student what else makes her feel the same way.

Often, the objectionable behavior may require the application of negative consequences to protect the learning process and ensure the safety of the student and others. Explain to the student that while you are working together to cement the replacement behavior, it is common for the old (objectionable) behavior to occur—but that once the student's need is effectively being met by the replacement behavior, the old behavior will cease. Explain why it is necessary to address the objectionable behavior with negative consequences during the transition period.

Even high school students can have a difficult time understanding how it is possible for someone (such as their teacher) to both actively help them learn a new behavior and still punish them. Children and young adults tend to think in black and white: "You are either my friend or my enemy." They may also not be used to being engaged by their teachers as partners to figure out how to change their behavior. Instead, they are used to adults either rewarding or punishing them in an attempt to control their behavior. In order to discipline troubled students, it is usually necessary that you first nurture them; establish a relationship of trust with them. Remember that the student's willingness (and often ability) to accept and benefit from your discipline is dependent on the maintenance of your relationship.

Environment-Based Tools

Definition

Any intervention that seeks to change behavior through thoughtful adaptations to environmental variables (such as physical setting, seat assignment, instructional level, presentation of instruction, assignment length, change of personnel, change of academic class order, provision of a verbal cue to initiate a replacement behavior, or provision of an in-class control center)

Environmental interventions manipulate what are usually referred to as *settings* and *setting events*. Following are some examples:

※ A student who is easily distracted receives a seat in close proximity to the teacher.

- A student who struggles to master the curriculum receives appropriate academic accommodations.

- A student who is challenged by math has her math class changed from seventh to first period to coincide with what she considers to be her most productive time of day.

- A student who has difficulty with self-control agrees to initiate a replacement behavior when his teacher uses a specified verbal cue (such as calling the student by his last name).

- A student who has difficulty accepting direction from her teacher agrees to choose between following her teacher's directive to stop teasing her classmate or taking 5 minutes in an "in-class control center," the designated area in the classroom where students go (by choice or direction) in order to regain control.

Often, environment-based tools are confused with skill-based tools. This is because what the adult does with an environment-based change tool (for example, creating an in-class control center) is linked to what the student does with a skill-based change tool (for example, applying a new skill or employing a more productive replacement behavior; choosing to stop the behavior or use the control center).

Things to Remember

Everything and everyone is part of the environment; think as broadly and as openly as possible. As stated earlier, don't just think outside of the box; be willing to build a *new* box. Just because the current situation is the way you experienced school, how you have always done it, or "how the best teachers do it," that is no reason to resist change if it will position your student to do better.

Consider what you and other adults are doing as both antecedents to and consequences of the student's behavior. Consider what should be done differently. Do it. Always look first at what you and other adults can do differently *before* looking at what the student should be doing differently. If an adult is stuck on a nonproductive behavior, consider the behavior's function, just as you would for a student. It can be both scary and rewarding to use the essential questions from chapter 5 (page 39) to aid in this endeavor. If you are really interested in changing the student's behavior, share the fact that you examined your own behavior first. This approach has proved very successful in buying even the most resistant of students into the process.

Consider whether or not the adults involved have the skills necessary to help the student change his or her behavior; if not, additional training is required. For example, a teacher may need to read an article or attend a training session on math accommodations, or a social worker may need to read an article or attend a training session on social stories. Again, there is absolutely nothing to lose and everything to gain by informing the student of what was done on his or her behalf, including that you or others sought professional development to better help the student.

Consider the school environment as a whole when developing an intervention plan. For example, if the student has had some anger management training as part of the plan, do the dean and principal know how to cue and facilitate the student's application of training strategies to real-life situations?

My experience with the development of individual behavior change plans has led me to the conclusion that all five behavior change tools have an important place in the teacher's toolbox for behavioral change. Be creative in your use of these tools!

The next chapter describes the five-step Plan to Do Better approach to put the tools to use and facilitate behavioral change.

Five Steps to Changing Behavior

He is the best sailor who can steer within fewest points of wind, and exact a motive power out of the greatest obstacles.

—Henry David Thoreau

Now that you understand the different kinds of intervention tools, this chapter will explain the five-step process for developing thoughtful, viable behavior change plans that incorporate those tools. This chapter also contains a collection of essential questions that serves as a useful resource for a problem-solving team engaged in developing behavior change plans. The questions provide thinking points and discussion prompts to help define the nonproductive behavior, secure the student's input, determine the function of the behavior, and select the appropriate behavior change tools.

Overview of the Plan to Do Better Process

Step 1: Identify and describe the nonproductive behavior,
including the behavior's characteristics and context.

Step 2: Secure the view, input, and suggestions of the student (required)
and parents or significant adults (recommended).

Step 3: Identify and describe the problem behavior's function(s),
and select the appropriate behavior change tool(s).

Step 4: Fully develop each of the selected tools.

Step 5: Develop and describe the behavior plan's assessment process and schedule.

The Plan to Do Better process does not include or require data collection in the form of direct student observation in order to define the problem behavior and to record information about its frequency, duration, and intensity. This is different from other, more rigid processes that are often associated with functional behavioral assessment (FBA) and special education. Plan to Do Better is primarily intended for use with general education students and *high-incidence* special education students—those with behavior disorders, emotional disturbances, and those with learning disabilities—who can communicate verbally and whose behavior (while troubling) is not deviant. These students typically do not exhibit aberrant behavior associated with some *low-incidence* developmentally delayed students; low-incidence behaviors include self-stimulation, self-mutilation, and talking to people who are not there.

School use of FBA that includes direct observation may be more applicable to low-incidence special education students. Researchers (Nelson et al., 1999) have questioned the need for FBA to be a part of all behavior change plans, in particular for students who do not have developmental disabilities; in this matter, public policy may have exceeded the existing research. Other researchers argue that "a tremendous amount of preventive work and interventions for simple behavior problems can be accomplished without the time and expense required to conduct an [FBA]" (Sugai et al., 1999, p. 253).

Today's schools face ever-increasing demands on time and human resources; decisions regarding both are always important. Plan to Do Better assumes that the student and the adults who interact daily with the student already have the information necessary to identify the problem behavior, discern its function, select the most potent behavior change tool(s), and develop a viable plan to change the student's behavior. A review of the student's records including (but not limited to) academic performance, intellectual ability, and discipline history should be completed, but rather than allocating more time for direct observation and data collection, the necessary individuals focus on discussing their information and developing a meaningful behavior change plan. A list of essential questions is included in this chapter to prompt personal reflection and team discussion; answering these questions will help uncover the information most critical to creating a successful Plan to Do Better.

Remember, Plan to Do Better differs from many similar processes for developing behavior change plans in that it views the student not as some*thing* to be worked *on*, but as some*one* to work *with*. Since the process is intended for use with students of average or better cognitive ability, securing their perspective on internal events is critical. Nicholas (2001) argues that much of the current thinking about the functional assessment of nonproductive behavior ignores internal events such as thoughts and feelings, and he advocates for assessment that accounts for intrapersonal variables associated with observable behavior. The Plan to Do Better process establishes the behavior's function through assessing both internal and external events. Accordingly, it requires student input and benefits from input from the student's parents or other significant adults.

Note: For a more scientific process and specific instruments for data collection (for example, direct and indirect assessment), please refer to *Dealing Effectively With Students Who Present Behavior Problems: The Functional Assessment of Behavior* (Van Acker, 1998). Van Acker's presentation is one of the most useful available.

The Office of Special Education Programs features a Positive Behavioral Interventions and Supports website, found at http://pbis.org; this is another useful resource.

The Plan to Do Better Process
Step 1

> Describe the nonproductive behavior, including the behavior's specific characteristics and context.

First, the team must define the presenting behavior (in other words, the behavior to be changed) in specific terms. Ambiguous terms like *aggressive behavior* should be translated into specific terms such as *hits* or *kicks*.

Most plans identify one or two behaviors to be changed. It can be difficult for the team to choose these behaviors, as some students present many undesirable behaviors. Select behaviors that, if changed, will have the most significant effect on the student's ability to succeed. The classroom teacher(s) and the student can help inform the selection by answering the following prompts:

※ *(Teacher)* "What one behavior, if changed, would position the student to be successful in your class?"

※ *(Student)* "What one behavior would you be most interested in changing?"

Unlike most behavior change processes, the Plan to Do Better process acknowledges that while identifying a specific behavior is necessary, that behavior is a *focus* point of intervention, not the *only* point of intervention. The team enters into the behavior change process considering the identified problem behavior, but understands that the actual plan will often address broader behavioral change. The sample plans provided in chapter 7 (page 79) help illustrate this distinction.

Table 5-1: Identifying Specific Behaviors

Presenting Behavior	Specific Behavior
Aggressive	Hits, kicks
Disruptive	Talks out, offers irrelevant comments
Tantrums	Cries, drops to the floor, goes limp, refuses the teacher's attempts to lift/ move

Next, the team must identify the behavior's *characteristics* (in other words, factors that increase or decrease the likelihood of the behavior occurring) and the behavior's *context* (the times and places the behavior is most and least likely to occur).

Table 5-2: Defining Characteristics and Context

Presenting Behavior	Specific Behavior	Specific Behavior With Characteristics and Context
Aggressive	Hits, kicks	Hits, kicks other students in unstructured activities during playground time
Disruptive	Talks out, offers irrelevant comments	Talks out of turn, making comments during math class such as "This is baby stuff" or "I learned this in second grade."
Tantrums	Cries, drops to the floor, goes limp, refuses the teacher's attempts to lift/move	Cries, drops to the floor, goes limp, refuses Mrs. Smith's attempts to lift/move. Behavior occurs whenever a limit on behavior is imposed (such as being required to complete seat work before using the computer).

Essential Questions

Discuss the following questions with the student's instructor(s) and others who have witnessed both the unproductive behavior and positive behaviors.

1. What specific conditions exist when the behavior is most and least likely to occur (for example, independent seat work, guided practice, whole group instruction, small group activities, or structured and unstructured activities)?

2. In what locations is the behavior most and least likely to occur (for example, in a classroom, lunchroom, hallway, or playground)?

3. When is the behavior most and least likely to occur (for example, upon arrival, just before dismissal, just prior to a specific subject, or during a specific subject or activity)?

4. What events or conditions occur prior to the onset of the behavior (such as transition to a specific subject, return from an out-of-class activity, request to perform a specific task, directive to limit or stop a behavior, or specific behavior of classmates)?

5. What are the consequences of the behavior? What happens immediately after the behavior occurs (such as the reaction of classmates, interaction with teacher, or removal from the classroom)?

6. What individuals (specific classmates, specific teachers, or a substitute teacher) are present when the behavior is most and least likely to occur?

7. What specific events or specific sets of circumstances happen simultaneously with the onset of the behavior (for example, a series of overcast days, repeated disappointments, teacher absence, and parental illness or absence)?

Step 2

Secure the view, input, and suggestions of the student (required) and parents or other significant adults (recommended).

Engage the student as a partner in the process. There is no better way to do this than to simply ask. Begin the conversation with general questions to help the student relax and to gain a better understanding of who the student is and how he or she feels about school. Ask specific questions regarding the problem behavior to discover the function(s) of the behavior and to guide selection of the necessary behavior change tool(s).

While the securing of the student's view is mandatory, it is often very helpful to also secure the views of parents or other significant adults. Not only does this provide additional information, it allows you to engage the parents in a collaborative effort to find solutions—to develop a plan for their child to do better. Refer to chapter 6 for a Standard Interview Form (page 52) and Parent or Guardian Survey (page 56).

Essential Questions

Discuss the following questions with the student. Be sure to explore both short-term and long-term consequences of the nonproductive behavior.

1. What do you really like about school?
2. What don't you like about school?
3. Is your work challenging? Do you find it too easy or too hard?
4. How do you feel about your teachers?
5. How do you think your teachers feel about you?
6. Do you have a lot of friends at school? Are any of them close friends?
7. In general, are you comfortable in school? Is there a specific time or place when you are uncomfortable?
8. What are you interested in, both in and out of school?
9. What are you good at, both in and out of school?
10. How do you spend your unscheduled time in and out of school?
11. What can you tell me about _____ BEHAVIOR ?
12. Do you know you are _____ BEHAVIOR when you're doing it?
13. Are you choosing to _____ BEHAVIOR ?
14. Can you stop _____ BEHAVIOR when you want to stop?
15. Can you stop _____ BEHAVIOR when you are asked to stop?
16. Do you know we have a rule against _____ BEHAVIOR ?
    Do you know why we have the rule?
17. Do you know what happens to students who _____ BEHAVIOR ?
18. Why do you do it?
19. What do you get out of doing it?
20. What do you avoid by doing it?
21. How do you feel when you do it?

Step 3

> Identify and describe the behavior's function(s), and select the appropriate behavior change tool(s).

Next, the team must integrate what they have learned from the student (and parents or significant adults) with what they already know in order to identify the function(s) of the problem behavior and to select the appropriate behavior change tool(s).

Note: In the event that the team can't determine the behavior's function or can't confidently select appropriate behavior change tools, the team may decide to conduct specific direct observation or a complete FBA.

Essential Questions

Discuss the following questions with the intervention team.

1. Is the student conscious of his or her behavior?

2. Is the nonproductive behavior under the student's control?

3. Does the student have a clear understanding of behavior expectations, rules, and the code of conduct in the school and/or classroom?

4. Is the student conscious of the short- and long-term consequences of his or her behavior?

5. Is the behavior intended to help the student achieve or receive something? If so, what?

6. Is the behavior intended to allow the student to avoid something? If so, what?

7. Does the student consider the consequences of the nonproductive behavior more rewarding than the consequences for an appropriate substitute behavior?

8. Is the student motivated to change his or her behavior and to engage in an appropriate substitute behavior?

9. How is the environment contributing to the maintenance of the problem behavior? What triggers it? What happens after the occurrence of the behavior to reinforce it?

10. How does the environment contribute to the maintenance of the nonproductive behavior? Have adults done everything possible to position the student to behave appropriately (by providing the student ample and varied opportunities to experience a sense of belonging, to be competent at what he or she is asked to do, to have some say in how he or she is asked to do it, and to look forward to having some fun on a regular basis)?

11. What is the relationship between the student's needs and the nonproductive behavior?

12. What is the relationship between the student's beliefs and the nonproductive behavior?

13. Are there additional internal variables interfacing with the problem behavior, such as emotions (anger, anxiety, frustration, depression, and so on)?

Step 4

> Fully develop *each* of the selected behavior change tools.

Next, the team must decide how to apply each of the selected behavior change tools (see chapter 4, or consult the following overview). Try to develop plans that incorporate several of the tools. Refer to chapter 7 (page 79) for examples of plans and demonstrations of how to apply the different tools.

Overview of the Behavior Change Tools

Reinforcement-Based Tools: Interventions that seek to change behavior through thoughtful manipulation of rewards and/or punishments

Belief-Based Tools: Interventions that seek to change behavior by helping the student to examine and discard disabling beliefs in favor of empowering ones

Skill-Based Tools: Interventions that seek to change behavior by teaching the student a specific skill or skill set necessary to the student successfully engaging in a productive replacement behavior

Needs-Based Tools: Interventions that seek to change behavior by identifying the basic need (to belong, to be competent, to experience independent choice, and to relax or have fun), and then providing the student with a replacement behavior that allows the student to gratify the identified need in a socially acceptable manner

Environment-Based Tools: Interventions that seek to change behavior through thoughtful adaptations to environmental variables (such as physical setting, seat assignment, instructional level, presentation of instruction, assignment length, change of academic class order, provision of a verbal cue to initiate a replacement behavior, or provision of an in-class control center)

Step 5

Develop and describe the behavior change plan's assessment process and schedule.

Finally, the team must develop a meaningful and practical assessment to determine whether the plan is working. The plan must include a schedule of assessment that indicates who is responsible for monitoring the assessment. Include a description of how assessment feedback will be provided to all stakeholders. Make every effort to include the student in the assessment process; by doing so, you continue to work *with*, not *on*, the student. This enhances your relationship with the student and positions the student to learn to self-monitor and ultimately internalize the behavior change.

Now that you know the five behavior change tools, the five-step process for applying them, and the essential questions to ask, the next chapter will provide the forms to help you create, record, and monitor the student's Plan to Do Better.

Chapter 6

Forms for Gathering Information

Seek first to understand, then to be understood.

—*Stephen Covey*

Visit **go.solution-tree.com/behavior**
to download all of these reproducibles.

All the interview, survey, questionnaire, inventory, and profile forms are intended to assist the behavior intervention team in the development of the behavior intervention plan.

This chapter contains the following forms to aid the team in its quest for relevant information:

- **Plan to Do Better**—This form is used to develop a record of the actual behavior intervention plan and to record the student's progress.

- **Standard Interview Form**—This is used to secure information from the behavior intervention team members or any individual the team believes has information relevant to the behavior and that may help answer essential questions.

- **Student Interview Form**—This form is used to secure information from the student; it may be completed by the student or by a team member who uses the form to record the student's responses.

- **Parent or Guardian Survey**—This is used to secure information from the parent or guardian; it may be completed by the parent or guardian, or by a team member who uses it to record the parent or guardian's responses.

- **Behavior Interview and Reinforcement Survey**—This form is used to secure information from the student regarding school, the nonproductive behavior, and what reinforces the student. Responses are recorded by the team member conducting the interview; the interview process itself is very important as it begins to enlist the student as an active participant.

- **Things My Teacher Should Know About Me: Interest Inventory for Elementary Students**—This is used to secure general information about the student; it may be completed by the student or by a team member who uses it to record the student's responses.

- **Things My Teacher Should Know About Me: Interest Inventory for Middle School Students**—This form is used to secure general information about the student; it may be completed by the student or by a team member who uses it to record the student's responses.

- **Things My Teacher Should Know About Me: Interest Inventory for High School Students**—This is used to secure general information about the student; it may be completed by the student or by a team member who uses it to record the student's responses.

- **Elementary School Survey**—This form is used to secure general information about the student through responses to open-ended prompts; it may be completed by the student or by a team member who uses it to record the student's responses.

- **Middle School Survey**—This form is used to secure general information about the student through responses to open-ended prompts; it may be completed by the student or by a team member who uses it to record the student's responses.

- **High School Survey**—This is used to secure general information about the student through responses to open-ended prompts; it may be completed by the student or by a team member who uses it to record the student's responses.

- **Elementary and Middle School Student Questionnaire**—This is used to secure student information regarding school; it may be completed by the student or by a team member who uses it to record the student's responses.

- **Junior High and High School Student Questionnaire**—This form secures student information regarding school; it may be completed by the student or by a team member who uses it to record the student's responses.

- **This Is Me**—This form secures general information about the student; it can be completed independently by the student or with the assistance of a team member.

- **Here I Am**—This form secures general information about the student; it can be completed independently by the student or with the assistance of a team member.

※ **I Prefer to Learn**—This form is used to secure information regarding the student's learning style and preference; it may be completed independently by the student or with the assistance of a team member.

※ **Teachers Who Help Me Succeed**—This form secures information regarding teacher behaviors preferred by the student; it may be completed independently by the student or with the assistance of a team member.

※ **Essential Questions**—These questions provide thinking points and discussion prompts to help facilitate the behavior change process.

Completed examples of the Plan to Do Better are detailed in chapter 7, which takes us through the process for four different students.

Plan to Do Better

Student _____ Grade____ School/Program/Class_____

Team Members

_____

_____

_____

_____

_____

_____

Date Initiated _____ Date Reviewed _____

• •

Description of Nonproductive Behavior, Including the Behavior's Specific Characteristics and Context

_____

_____

_____

_____

View, Input, and Suggestions of the Student (Required) and Parents or Significant Adults (Recommended)

_____

_____

_____

_____

Description of the Function(s) of the Behavior

_____

_____

_____

_____

Selection and Development of Behavior Change Tool(s)

☐ Reinforcement-Based Tools

_____

_____

_____

_____

continued on next page→

Plan to Do Better (Cont'd)

☐ Belief-Based Tools

_____
_____
_____
_____

☐ Skill-Based Tools

_____
_____
_____
_____

☐ Needs-Based Tools

_____
_____
_____
_____

☐ Environment-Based Tools

_____
_____
_____
_____

Description of the Behavior Change Plan's Assessment (Process and Schedule)

_____
_____
_____
_____

Other Notes

_____
_____
_____
_____

Standard Interview Form

Name _____ Date of Interview _____

Respondent _____

Interviewer _____

1. Describe the nonproductive behavior.

   _____

   _____

   _____

   _____

   _____

   _____

   _____

   _____

2. How often does the behavior occur?

   _____

   _____

   _____

   _____

3. How long does it last?

   _____

   _____

   _____

   _____

4. How intense is the behavior?

   _____

   _____

   _____

   _____

5. What happens just prior to the behavior occurring?

   _____

   _____

   _____

   _____

continued on next page→

Standard Interview Form (Cont'd)

6. What is happening when the behavior occurs?

_____

_____

_____

_____

7. When is the behavior most and least likely to occur?

_____

_____

_____

_____

8. Where is the behavior most and least likely to occur?

_____

_____

_____

_____

9. With whom is the behavior most and least likely to occur?

_____

_____

_____

_____

10. What conditions are most likely to set off the behavior?

_____

_____

_____

_____

11. Are there cues that indicate the behavior is about to start? If so, what are they?

_____

_____

_____

_____

continued on next page→

Standard Interview Form (Cont'd)

12. What happens after the behavior occurs? Describe how the teacher, other adults, and peers respond.

_____

_____

_____

_____

13. What is the likely function(s) of the behavior? What does the student get or avoid?

_____

_____

_____

_____

14. What productive and socially acceptable behavior(s) might serve the same function?

_____

_____

_____

_____

15. Who do you think could contribute to developing and implementing this student's intervention plan?

_____

_____

_____

_____

16. What other information do you want to share?

_____

_____

_____

_____

Student Interview Form

Name_____ Date of Interview _____

Interviewer _____

Circle the appropriate answer.

1. Is your teacher trying hard to help you learn?	Always	Sometimes	Never
2. Is your teacher trying hard to help you behave responsibly?	Always	Sometimes	Never
3. Does your teacher value your opinion?	Always	Sometimes	Never
4. Does your teacher know when you don't understand something?	Always	Sometimes	Never
5. Is your work interesting?	Always	Sometimes	Never
6. Is your work too hard for you?	Always	Sometimes	Never
7. Is your work too easy for you?	Always	Sometimes	Never
8. In general, do you feel respected?	Always	Sometimes	Never
9. Does your teacher let you know when you do a good job?	Always	Sometimes	Never
10. Do you get help when you need it?	Always	Sometimes	Never
11. In general, do you have enough input into how your instruction is presented?	Always	Sometimes	Never
12. In general, does your teacher adjust your instruction to make it easier for you to learn?	Always	Sometimes	Never
13. Do you think your work periods (subjects and classes) are reasonable lengths of time?	Always	Sometimes	Never
14. In general, are you comfortable with your peers?	Always	Sometimes	Never
15. In general, are you able to relax?	Always	Sometimes	Never
16. In general, are you able to concentrate?	Always	Sometimes	Never
17. In general, do you understand your teachers?	Always	Sometimes	Never
18. In general, can you follow your teacher's lectures?	Always	Sometimes	Never
19. In general, are your notes helpful in preparing for quizzes and tests?	Always	Sometimes	Never
20. Do you spend enough time studying?	Always	Sometimes	Never
21. In general, is homework useful in helping you to better understand class work?	Always	Sometimes	Never
22. Are grades motivating to you?	Always	Sometimes	Never
23. Do you think you would do better if you received more rewards for working hard?	Always	Sometimes	Never
24. In general, does showing up, behaving right, and working hard equal success?	Always	Sometimes	Never
25. When you go to school, do you expect to have some fun in your day?	Always	Sometimes	Never

Parent or Guardian Survey

Student Name _____

Parent Name _____ Date_____

Please answer the following questions to help us teach your child in the best way that he or she learns. Thank you!

1. Describe your child's personality. _____
   _____
   _____
   _____

2. Can your child switch from one activity   Yes   No   Sometimes
   to another easily? (Circle one.)

3. What kinds of activities are easy for your child?_____
   _____
   _____
   _____

4. What kinds of activities are hard for your child?_____
   _____
   _____
   _____

5. What has your child done that makes you proud?_____
   _____
   _____
   _____

6. What has your child done that makes you upset?_____
   _____
   _____
   _____

7. Did your child have learning or behavioral difficulties   Yes   No
   before the age of 5? (Circle one.)

8. Does your child have any special talents?_____
   _____
   _____
   _____

continued on next page→

Parent or Guardian Survey (Cont'd)

9. What specific problems did you notice your child experiencing? _____

_____

_____

_____

10. Does your child make plans with friends in advance? _____

_____

_____

_____

11. Does your child have friends in the community? (Circle one.)   Yes   No   Sometimes

12. What has the school done that has been the most helpful? _____

_____

_____

_____

13. What could the school do that would be helpful to you in the future? _____

_____

_____

_____

14. What does your child like and dislike about school? _____

_____

_____

_____

15. What has been the most stressful part of being a parent or guardian of your child? _____

_____

_____

_____

16. Has your child received any services outside of school, such as speech therapy, counseling, tutoring, testing, or others? (Circle one.)   Yes   No

17. Which family member(s) does your child enjoy spending time with at home? _____

_____

_____

_____

continued on next page→

Parent or Guardian Survey (Cont'd)

18. What activities does your child like to do at home? _____

_____

_____

_____

19. What activities at home does your child dislike doing? _____

_____

_____

_____

20. What foods or snacks does your child like? Dislike? _____

_____

_____

_____

21. Does your child do chores and work at home   Yes   No   Sometimes
without reminders? (Circle one.)

22. Does your child misplace or lose his or her belongings,   Yes   No   Sometimes
including favorite ones? (Circle one.)

23. Does your child remember to bring books and materials   Yes   No   Sometimes
needed to do homework? (Circle one.)

24. Does your child need help when doing homework? (Circle one.)   Yes   No   Sometimes

25. Which method of communication with the school do you prefer? (Circle your answer.)
Phone calls   Notes   Progress reports   Email

Other _____

_____

_____

_____

Behavior Interview and Reinforcement Survey

Student Name _____ Grade _____ Birthdate _____

Person Facilitating the Interview _____ Date of Interview _____

Section 1

Ask the student the following questions and circle the appropriate answers.

1. In general, is your work too hard for you?	Always	Sometimes	Never
2. In general, is your work too easy for you?	Always	Sometimes	Never
3. When you ask for help appropriately, do you get it?	Always	Sometimes	Never
4. Do you think work periods for each subject are too long?	Always	Sometimes	Never
5. Do you think work periods for each subject are too short?	Always	Sometimes	Never
6. When you work at your desk, do you do better when someone works with you?	Always	Sometimes	Never
7. Do you think people notice when you do a good job?	Always	Sometimes	Never
8. Do you think you get the points or rewards you deserve when you do good work?	Always	Sometimes	Never
9. Do you think you would do better in school if you received more rewards?	Always	Sometimes	Never
10. In general, do you find your work interesting?	Always	Sometimes	Never
11. Are there things in the classroom that distract you?	Always	Sometimes	Never
12. Is your work challenging enough?	Always	Sometimes	Never

Section 2

Ask the student the specific questions for the nonproductive behavior and record the answers given.

List the nonproductive behavior: _____

_____

_____

When do you think you have the fewest problems with this behavior?_____

_____

_____

When do you think you have the most problems with this behavior?_____

_____

_____

Why do you have problems during these times?_____

_____

_____

continued on next page→

Behavior Interview and Reinforcement Survey (Cont'd)

What changes could be made so that you have fewer problems with this behavior? _____

_____

_____

Section 3

Ask the student to rate how much he or she likes each of the subjects you will read aloud. Please circle the student's answers.

Reading	Not at All	Fair	Very Much
Math	Not at All	Fair	Very Much
Spelling	Not at All	Fair	Very Much
Handwriting	Not at All	Fair	Very Much
Science	Not at All	Fair	Very Much
Social Studies	Not at All	Fair	Very Much
English/Language Arts	Not at All	Fair	Very Much
Music	Not at All	Fair	Very Much
Physical Education	Not at All	Fair	Very Much
Art	Not at All	Fair	Very Much
Other (please list subject)	Not at All	Fair	Very Much

Section 4

Ask the student to complete the following statements, and write down their answers.

1. My favorite adult at school is: _____

   The things I like to do with this adult are: _____

   _____

   _____

2. My best friend at school is: _____

   Some things I like to do with my best friend at school are: _____

   _____

   _____

3. Some other friends I have at school are: _____

   Some things I like to do with them are: _____

   _____

   _____

continued on next page→

Behavior Interview and Reinforcement Survey (Cont'd)

4. When I do well in school, a person I'd like to know about it is: _____

5. When I do well in school, I wish my teacher would: _____

6. At school, I'd like to spend more time with: _____

    Some things I'd like to do with this person are: _____

    _____

    _____

7. One thing I'd really like to do more in school is: _____

8. When I have free time at school, I like to: _____

9. I feel great in school when: _____

10. The person who likes me best at school is: _____

    I think this person likes me because: _____

11. I will do almost anything to keep from: _____

12. The kind of punishment at school that I hate most is: _____

13. I sure get mad at school when I can't: _____

14. The thing that upsets my teacher the most is: _____

15. The thing that upsets me the most is: _____

Favorite Edible Reinforcers

Read the following list of reinforcers to the student, and check all that apply.
Ask the student, "Which of the following would you like to be rewarded with?"

☐ Candy (Specify) _____   ☐ Snacks (Specify) _____

☐ Fruit (Specify) _____   ☐ Nuts (Specify) _____

☐ Drinks (Specify) _____   ☐ Vegetables (Specify) _____

☐ Cereal (Specify) _____   ☐ Other (Specify) _____

continued on next page→

Behavior Interview and Reinforcement Survey (Cont'd)

Favorite Academic Reinforcers

Read the following list of reinforcers to students, and check all that apply.
Ask the student, "Which of the following would you like to be rewarded with?"

☐ Going to the library

☐ Having good work displayed

☐ Getting good grades

☐ Having parents praise good schoolwork

☐ Giving reports

☐ Making projects

☐ Completing creative writing projects

☐ Earning teacher praise

☐ Helping grade papers

☐ Getting a good note sent home

☐ Other (Specify) _____

Favorite Tangible Items

Read the following list of reinforcers to students, and check all that apply.
Ask the student, "Which of the following items would you like to be rewarded with?"

☐ Stuffed animals

☐ Pencils, markers, crayons

☐ Paper

☐ Trucks, tractors

☐ Sports equipment

☐ Toys

☐ Books

☐ Puzzles

☐ Other (Specify) _____

Favorite Social Reinforcers

Read the following list of reinforcers to students, and check all that apply.
Ask the student, "Which of the following makes you feel rewarded?"

☐ Teaching things to other people

☐ Being the teacher's helper

☐ Spending time with friends

☐ Spending time with the teacher

☐ Spending time with the principal

☐ Spending time with _____

☐ Having class parties

☐ Working with friends in class

☐ Helping keep the room clean

☐ Being a tutor

☐ Being a leader in class

☐ Other (Specify) _____

continued on next page→

Behavior Interview and Reinforcement Survey (Cont'd)

Favorite Recreation and Leisure Reinforcers

Read the following list of reinforcers to students, and check all that apply. Ask the student, "Which of the following recreational opportunities would you like to be rewarded with?"

☐ Using the computer

☐ Listening to music

☐ Singing

☐ Playing a musical instrument

☐ Watching TV

☐ Cooking

☐ Building models

☐ Woodworking and carpentry

☐ Sports (Specify) _____

☐ Working with crafts

☐ Other (Specify) _____

☐ Other (Specify) _____

Things My Teacher Should Know About Me

Interest Inventory for Elementary Students

Student Name _____ Date _____

Please help me find out about some of the things you like by answering the following questions. Thank you.

1. WHO would you like to spend some free time with?

   Names of kids: _____

   _____

   Names of teachers and adults: _____

   _____

2. WHAT do you like to do at recess or during your free time in school?

   Games: _____

   _____

   Sports you like to play: _____

   _____

   Other things: _____

   _____

   _____

3. WHEN do you learn best at school? (Please circle your answer.) Morning Midday Afternoon

4. WHAT is your favorite T.V. show? _____

5. WHAT are a few of your favorite movies? _____

   _____

6. WHAT do you like to eat for a snack? _____

7. WHAT do you like to do with your friends after school? _____

   _____

8. WHERE do you like to go with your family? _____

9. WHO do you like to spend time with the most in your family? _____

   _____

Things My Teachers Should Know About Me

Interest Inventory for Middle School Students

Student Name _____ Date _____

Please help your teachers find out about some of the things you like by answering the following questions. Thank you!

1. What are your favorite classes in school? _____
   _____

2. Who is your favorite teacher or adult at school? _____

3. What activities or clubs do you belong to or participate in at school? _____
   _____

   In your community? _____
   _____

4. What sports do you like to play? _____

5. Who is your favorite sports team? _____

6. What do you like to do in your free time at school? _____
   _____

7. What are some of your favorite books? _____

8. What are your hobbies? _____

9. What kind of music do you listen to? _____

10. Who is your favorite singer or band? _____

11. What type of movies do you like to watch? _____

12. What do you like to do with your free time after school? _____
    _____

13. What do you like to do with your family? _____
    _____

14. Which people in your family do you like to spend your free time with? _____

15. What types of food do you like to eat for a snack? _____

16. What do you like to do during vacations? _____
    _____

Things My Teachers Should Know About Me
Interest Inventory for High School Students

Student Name _____ Date _____

Please help your teachers find out about some of the things you like by answering the following questions. Thank you!

1. What are your favorite classes in school? _____
   _____

2. Who are your favorite teachers? _____

3. What activities do your favorite teachers use to make learning interesting? _____
   _____

4. What activities or clubs do you belong to or participate in at school? _____
   _____

   In your community? _____
   _____

5. What is your favorite sport? _____
   To play? _____
   To watch? _____

6. What type of movies do you like to watch? _____
   _____

7. What kind of music do you listen to? _____

8. Who is your favorite singer or band? _____

9. What do you like to do with your friends after school? _____
   _____

10. What do you like to do with your family on the weekends? _____
    _____

11. Which people in your family do you like to spend time with? _____

12. What do you like to spend money on? _____
    _____

13. What are your hobbies or special interests? _____
    _____

Behave Yourself! © 2009 Solution Tree • www.solution-tree.com
Visit **go.solution-tree.com/behavior** to download this form.

Elementary School Survey

Name _____ Date _____

Please finish the sentences so that your teacher can get to know you better. Thank you!

1. I get mad when: _____

   _____

   _____

2. My teacher wants me to: _____

   _____

   _____

3. I am happy when: _____

   _____

   _____

4. At recess I like to: _____

   _____

   _____

5. The person I like the most is: _____

6. The person who upsets me is: _____

7. My friends and I like to: _____

   _____

   _____

8. I get in trouble when: _____

   _____

9. Homework is: _____

   _____

10. I want my teacher to: _____

    _____

    _____

11. After school I: _____

    _____

    _____

12. At night I: _____

    _____

    _____

Middle School Survey

Name _____ Date _____

Please finish the sentences so that your teacher(s) can learn more about you. Thank you!

1. The thing that makes me mad is: _____

   _____

2. I feel upset or worried when: _____

   _____

3. I get in trouble because: _____

   _____

4. The person I like best is: _____

5. I am really happy when: _____

   _____

6. My teacher(s) want me to: _____

   _____

7. My friends say: _____

   _____

8. I find it hard to: _____

   _____

9. I find it easy to: _____

   _____

10. I could do better if: _____

    _____

11. I would like my teacher to: _____

    _____

12. My best subject is: _____

13. Homework is: _____

    _____

14. I would like my family to: _____

    _____

15. At night I like to: _____

    _____

16. My chores at home are: _____

    _____

High School Survey

Name _____ Date _____

Please complete this survey to help your teacher(s) learn about your likes and dislikes. Thank you!

1. What subject(s) in school do you find interesting? _____
   _____

2. What subject(s) in school are not interesting? _____
   _____

3. What clubs or activities do you participate in at school? _____

4. What neighborhood activities do you participate in? _____

5. Do you like to play sports, watch them, or both? _____
   What sports do you play in school? _____

6. If you like sports, which team or athlete is your favorite? _____

7. What do you like to do after school? _____
   _____

8. What kinds of movies do you like? _____
   What are some of your favorite movies? _____
   _____

9. Do you like to read? _____ What are some of your favorite books? _____
   _____

10. Which TV shows do you watch? _____

11. What do you like to do after school? _____
   _____

12. What do you like to do on the weekends? _____
   _____

13. Do you have a part-time job? _____ If yes, what do you do? _____

14. How many hours a week do you work? _____

15. What chores are you expected to do at home? _____

16. Where do you like to go to eat with your friends? _____

17. What do you want to do after graduating from high school? _____
   _____

18. What kind of job do you want after high school? _____

Elementary and Middle School Student Questionnaire

Name _____ Date _____

This will help us understand how you learn. It will help you learn better and help me teach better. Put a check next to the one that tells the way you learn.

When I am in class . . .

1. I use an assignment notebook.	☐ Yes	☐ No	☐ Sometimes
2. I bring the things I need to class.	☐ Yes	☐ No	☐ Sometimes
3. I raise my hand before I speak.	☐ Yes	☐ No	☐ Sometimes
4. I can stay in my seat.	☐ Yes	☐ No	☐ Sometimes
5. I like to read out loud.	☐ Yes	☐ No	☐ Sometimes
6. I start my work without help.	☐ Yes	☐ No	☐ Sometimes
7. I like to work in a group.	☐ Yes	☐ No	☐ Sometimes
8. I ask the teacher for help when work is hard for me.	☐ Yes	☐ No	☐ Sometimes
9. I finish my work on time.	☐ Yes	☐ No	☐ Sometimes
10. I bring home the things I need to do my homework.	☐ Yes	☐ No	☐ Sometimes

When I do homework . . .

1. I do my homework without any help.	☐ Yes	☐ No	☐ Sometimes
2. I know how long it will take me to do my work.	☐ Yes	☐ No	☐ Sometimes
3. I know how to study from books.	☐ Yes	☐ No	☐ Sometimes
4. I remember what we talked about in school.	☐ Yes	☐ No	☐ Sometimes
5. I hand in my homework on time.	☐ Yes	☐ No	☐ Sometimes
6. I read directions carefully.	☐ Yes	☐ No	☐ Sometimes
7. I learn new words quickly.	☐ Yes	☐ No	☐ Sometimes
8. I understand what I read.	☐ Yes	☐ No	☐ Sometimes

When I take tests . . .

1. I get upset when I take a test.	☐ Yes	☐ No	☐ Sometimes
2. I understand the questions on the test.	☐ Yes	☐ No	☐ Sometimes
3. I have trouble with true and false tests.	☐ Yes	☐ No	☐ Sometimes
4. I have trouble with multiple-choice tests.	☐ Yes	☐ No	☐ Sometimes
5. I have trouble writing short answers for a test.	☐ Yes	☐ No	☐ Sometimes
6. I remember to use capital letters and punctuation.	☐ Yes	☐ No	☐ Sometimes
7. I remember what I studied.	☐ Yes	☐ No	☐ Sometimes
8. I finish tests on time.	☐ Yes	☐ No	☐ Sometimes

Junior High and High School Student Questionnaire

Name _____ Date _____

The purpose of this questionnaire is to help you to understand how you learn and how to use your learning strengths to improve areas of difficulty. Put a check next to the one that tells the way you learn.

When I organize my work . . .

I use an assignment book or calendar.	☐ Yes	☐ No	☐ Sometimes
I forget to bring things I need to class.	☐ Yes	☐ No	☐ Sometimes
I can find assignments, books, or notes.	☐ Yes	☐ No	☐ Sometimes
I forget to bring home things I need for homework and studying.	☐ Yes	☐ No	☐ Sometimes
I know how long it will take me to do my work.	☐ Yes	☐ No	☐ Sometimes

When I study . . .

I know how to start studying.	☐ Yes	☐ No	☐ Sometimes
I can pay attention.	☐ Yes	☐ No	☐ Sometimes
I can remember what I learned in class.	☐ Yes	☐ No	☐ Sometimes
I find it hard to study from books.	☐ Yes	☐ No	☐ Sometimes
I know how to remember information for tests.	☐ Yes	☐ No	☐ Sometimes

When I read . . .

I forget vocabulary words I learned.	☐ Yes	☐ No	☐ Sometimes
I can understand difficult words.	☐ Yes	☐ No	☐ Sometimes
I read slowly.	☐ Yes	☐ No	☐ Sometimes
I have difficulty understanding what I read.	☐ Yes	☐ No	☐ Sometimes
I have trouble understanding the main idea.	☐ Yes	☐ No	☐ Sometimes

When I write . . .

I have trouble spelling.	☐ Yes	☐ No	☐ Sometimes
I find it hard to remember to use correct capitalization.	☐ Yes	☐ No	☐ Sometimes
I have trouble writing good sentences.	☐ Yes	☐ No	☐ Sometimes
I have trouble finding and correcting my mistakes.	☐ Yes	☐ No	☐ Sometimes
I find it hard to organize my words.	☐ Yes	☐ No	☐ Sometimes

continued on next page →

Junior High and High School
Student Questionnaire (Cont'd)

When I take tests . . .

I read the directions carefully.	☐ Yes	☐ No	☐ Sometimes
I understand the directions or questions on the test.	☐ Yes	☐ No	☐ Sometimes
I get very nervous.	☐ Yes	☐ No	☐ Sometimes
I can remember what I studied.	☐ Yes	☐ No	☐ Sometimes
I have difficulty finishing tests on time.	☐ Yes	☐ No	☐ Sometimes
I have difficulty with essay questions.	☐ Yes	☐ No	☐ Sometimes
I have difficulty with multiple-choice questions.	☐ Yes	☐ No	☐ Sometimes
I have difficulty with true/false questions.	☐ Yes	☐ No	☐ Sometimes

When I am in class . . .

I have trouble paying attention.	☐ Yes	☐ No	☐ Sometimes
I find it hard to listen and take notes.	☐ Yes	☐ No	☐ Sometimes
I forget to raise my hand to speak.	☐ Yes	☐ No	☐ Sometimes
I like to read out loud.	☐ Yes	☐ No	☐ Sometimes
I like to be called on.	☐ Yes	☐ No	☐ Sometimes
I have trouble staying in my seat.	☐ Yes	☐ No	☐ Sometimes
I have a hard time starting an assignment.	☐ Yes	☐ No	☐ Sometimes
I have a hard time working without help.	☐ Yes	☐ No	☐ Sometimes
I find it hard to work in a group.	☐ Yes	☐ No	☐ Sometimes
I have a hard time asking the teacher for help.	☐ Yes	☐ No	☐ Sometimes
I know what questions to ask the teacher.	☐ Yes	☐ No	☐ Sometimes
I have a hard time finishing my work on time.	☐ Yes	☐ No	☐ Sometimes

This Is Me

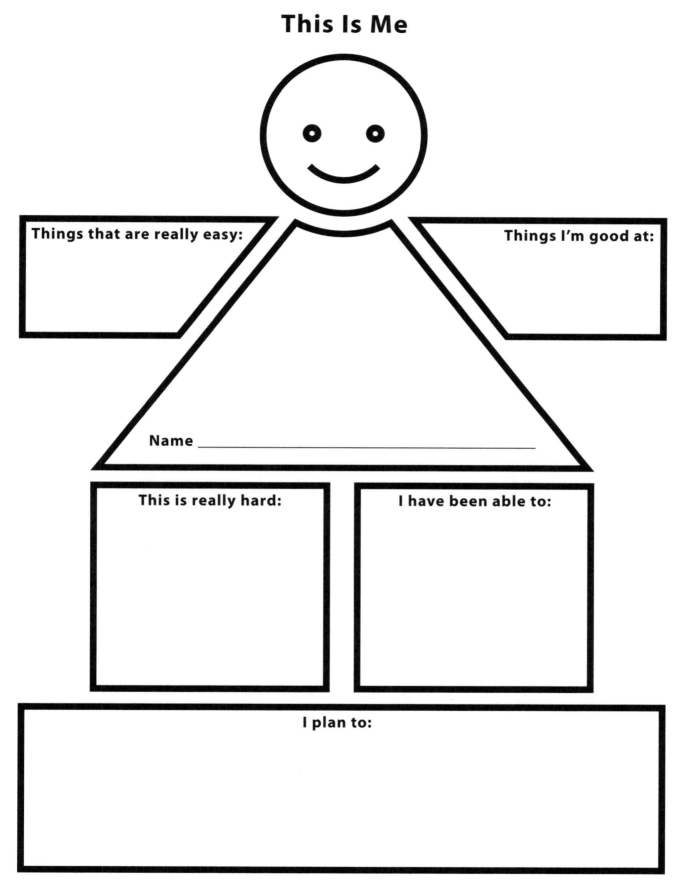

Things that are really easy:

Things I'm good at:

Name _____

This is really hard:

I have been able to:

I plan to:

Here I Am

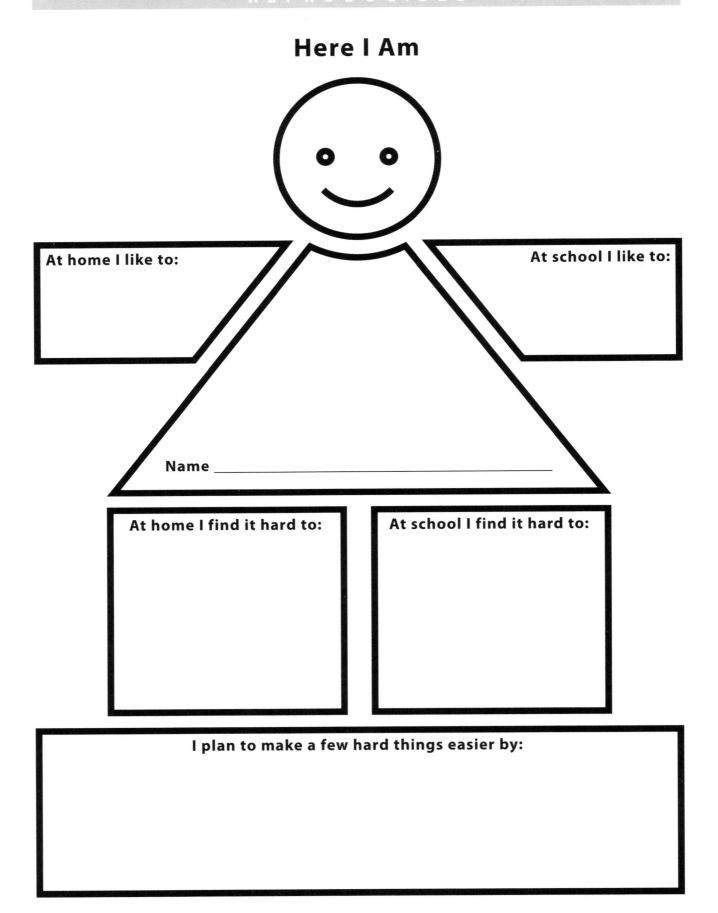

At home I like to:

At school I like to:

Name _____

At home I find it hard to:

At school I find it hard to:

I plan to make a few hard things easier by:

I Prefer to Learn

Name _____ Date _____

Activities

Rank the following from 1 to 8, with 1 being your most preferred and 8 your least preferred.

_____ Reading   _____ Completing worksheets   _____ Making oral reports
_____ Listening   _____ Completing study guides   _____ Taking notes
_____ Discussing   _____ Writing reports   _____ Other

Resources

Rank the following from 1 to 8, with 1 being the learning resource you use most and 8 being the one you use least.

_____ Dictionary   _____ Notes or note cards   _____ Study guides
_____ Computer   _____ Tape recorder   _____ Graphic organizers
_____ Calculator   _____ Films or videos   _____ Other

Rank the following from 1 to 4, with 1 being the setting in which you learn best and 4 being the setting in which you learn worst.

_____ Large group   _____ Independently   _____ Other
_____ Small group   _____ One-to-one tutoring

Rank the following from 1 to 5, with 1 being the way you most prefer to be tested and 5 the way you least prefer to be tested.

_____ Multiple choice   _____ Essay   _____ Orally
_____ Short answer   _____ Open book   _____ Other

Teachers Who Help Me Succeed

Name _____ Date _____

Please write your answers to the following questions.

1. Teachers I learn the most from always: _____
   _____
   _____

2. Teachers I learn the most from never: _____
   _____

3. Teachers really make me feel included when they: _____
   _____
   _____

4. Teachers make me want to work hard when they: _____
   _____
   _____

5. Teachers make me feel like I can succeed at the things that don't come easy to me when they:
   _____
   _____

6. Teachers help me to act responsibly when they: _____
   _____
   _____

7. Teachers help me get back on task when they: _____
   _____

8. Teachers make it easy for me to handle criticism when they: _____
   _____

9. Teachers make it easy for me to take correction when they: _____
   _____

10. Teachers show me I am important when they: _____
    _____
    _____

11. The teacher I learn most from: _____
    _____

12. The teacher I had the most fun with: _____
    _____

Behave Yourself! © 2009 Solution Tree • www.solution-tree.com
Visit **go.solution-tree.com/behavior** to download this form.

Essential Questions

Defining and Refining Nonproductive Behaviors

Discuss the following questions with the student's instructor(s) and others who have witnessed both the unproductive behavior and positive behaviors.

1. What specific conditions exist when the behavior is most and least likely to occur (for example, independent seat work, guided practice, whole group instruction, small group activities, or structured and unstructured activities)?

2. In what locations is the behavior most and least likely to occur (for example, in a classroom, lunchroom, hallway, or playground)?

3. When is the behavior most and least likely to occur (for example, upon arrival, just before dismissal, just prior to a specific subject, or during a specific subject or activity)?

4. What events or conditions occur prior to the onset of the behavior (such as transition to a specific subject, return from an out-of-class activity, request to perform a specific task, directive to limit or stop a behavior, or specific behavior of classmates)?

5. What are the consequences of the behavior? What happens immediately after the behavior occurs (such as the reaction of classmates, interaction with teacher, or removal from the classroom)?

6. What individuals (specific classmates, specific teachers, or a substitute teacher) are present when the behavior is most and least likely to occur?

7. What specific events or specific sets of circumstances happen simultaneously with the onset of the behavior (for example, a series of overcast days, repeated disappointments, teacher absence, and parental illness or absence)?

Securing the Student's View, Input, and Suggestions

Discuss the following questions with the student. Be sure to explore both short-term and long-term consequences of the nonproductive behavior.

1. What do you really like about school?

2. What don't you like about school?

3. Is your work challenging? Do you find it too easy or too hard?

4. How do you feel about your teachers?

5. How do you think your teachers feel about you?

6. Do you have a lot of friends at school? Are any of them close friends?

7. In general, are you comfortable in school? Is there a specific time or place when you are uncomfortable?

8. What are you interested in, both in and out of school?

9. What are you good at, both in and out of school?

10. How do you spend your unscheduled time in and out of school?

11. What can you tell me about _____?
    <small>BEHAVIOR</small>

continued on next page→

Essential Questions (Cont'd)

12. Do you know you are _____ when you're doing it?
    <small>BEHAVIOR</small>

13. Are you choosing to _____ ?
    <small>BEHAVIOR</small>

14. Can you stop _____ when you want to stop?
    <small>BEHAVIOR</small>

15. Can you stop _____ when you are asked to stop?
    <small>BEHAVIOR</small>

16. Do you know we have a rule against _____ ?
    <small>BEHAVIOR</small>
    Do you know why we have the rule?

17. Do you know what happens to students who _____ ?
    <small>BEHAVIOR</small>

18. Why do you do it?

19. What do you get out of doing it?

20. What do you avoid by doing it?

21. How do you feel when you do it?

Determining the Function of the Nonproductive Behavior and Selecting the Most Effective Behavior Change Tools

Discuss the following questions with the intervention team.

1. Is the student conscious of his or her behavior?

2. Is the nonproductive behavior under the student's control?

3. Does the student have a clear understanding of behavior expectations, rules, and the code of conduct in the school and/or classroom?

4. Is the student conscious of the short- and long-term consequences of his or her behavior?

5. Is the behavior intended to help the student achieve or receive something? If so, what?

6. Is the behavior intended to allow the student to avoid something? If so, what?

7. Does the student consider the consequences of the nonproductive behavior more rewarding than the consequences for an appropriate substitute behavior?

8. Is the student motivated to change his or her behavior and to engage in an appropriate substitute behavior?

9. How is the environment contributing to the maintenance of the problem behavior? What triggers it? What happens after the occurrence of the behavior to reinforce it?

10. How does the environment contribute to the maintenance of the nonproductive behavior? Have adults done everything possible to position the student to behave appropriately (by providing the student ample and varied opportunities to experience a sense of belonging, to be competent at what he or she is asked to do, to have some say in how he or she is asked to do it, and to look forward to having some fun on a regular basis)?

11. What is the relationship between the student's needs and the nonproductive behavior?

12. What is the relationship between the student's beliefs and the nonproductive behavior?

13. Are there additional internal variables interfacing with the problem behavior, such as emotions (anger, anxiety, frustration, depression, and so on)?

Chapter 7

Sample Behavior Change Plans

Setting an example is not the main means of influencing another; it is the only means.

—*Albert Einstein*

This chapter provides four examples of Plans to Do Better to illustrate how a problem-solving team may use the process and the tools this book offers.

Each plan includes a description of the problem behavior, a statement of the student's view of the behavior and situation, and a description of the problem behavior's function. Also included are the specific behavior change tools the team selected and developed. Each plan also contains a method and schedule for assessing the plan's effectiveness. Finally, each plan includes a summary of the team's answers to the essential questions (see page 77)—used to make decisions and develop the plan—and a list of the resources used in the exercise.

The sample plans center around four fictional students:

- ⁂ Terri is a third-grade general education student who blurts out irrelevant, silly comments and is in danger of being referred for a special education evaluation.

- ⁂ Jarrel is a sixth-grade general education student who is both verbally and physically aggressive.

- ⁂ Tommy is an eighth-grade self-contained student with a behavioral disorder who bullies his classmates.

- ⁂ Nick is a 10th-grade general education student who is insubordinate and disrespectful to adults. He is also performing below his academic potential.

Plan to Do Better

Student _Terri Logan_   **Grade** _3rd_   **School/Program/Class** _General education_

Team Members

Ms. Williams, classroom teacher

Ms. Van, psychologist

Mr. Todd, intervention specialist

Mr. Denst, social worker

Mrs. Morgan, director of special education and pre-referral coordinator

Mrs. Smith, special education resource teacher

Mrs. Morgantini, principal

Mrs. Logan, mother

Date Initiated _10/22/05_   **Date Reviewed** _____

. . . .

Description of Nonproductive Behavior, Including the Behavior's Specific Characteristics and Context

Terri makes silly and irrelevant comments that are disruptive to class and to Terri's skill acquisition. Terri's comments are almost exclusively contained to language arts instruction and assignments that necessitate grade level reading skills. The behavior occurs in direct instruction, small group instruction, and cooperative learning group work. It does not occur during individual seatwork. The problem behavior usually responds to redirection. If not, Terri sits in the classroom control center for a few minutes and then returns to class. Terri's comments usually receive some laughter from her classmates.

View, Input, and Suggestions of the Student (Required) and Parents or Significant Adults (Recommended)

Terri was interviewed by Mr. Denst in several 20–30 minute meetings. Terri indicated that she liked school, her teachers, and her classmates. Terri said she had lots of friends and named two special friends. She was very eager to let Mr. Denst know that she tries hard, but that she is just not as smart as a lot of the other kids. She said reading instruction and assignments were not too hard, but she said she did not like reading or having to read long things. She did not offer much regarding why she blurts out during class, only that sometimes she is bored and feels like everyone is looking at her, so she feels like she has to do something. She did not realize that the behavior is almost always during reading instruction or related activities. When asked, Terri said she wants to be good. She said math is her favorite class and that she is good at it, but not as good as her brother. Her favorite things to do outside of school are playing outside and playing with her Barbie.

Mr. and Mrs. Logan indicated through their responses to the Parent or Guardian Survey that they are very concerned about the disruptive behavior. They also made it known that Terri had similar problems at her previous school and that she has always had learning difficulties related to reading (Terri transferred in at the start of third grade). They also shared that they believe Terri is somewhat intimidated by her older brother and sister, who have always done extremely well in school. When quizzed about Terri's strengths, they said she has a wonderful voice, loves to sing, and is very coordinated for her age. Mrs. Logan participated in the team meeting to develop the Plan to Do Better.

Description of the Function(s) of the Behavior

The behavior's primary function is to restore a feeling of well-being when Terri is feeling nervous or embarrassed during reading instruction, or during other activities that tax her reading skills. The behavior also results in attention from her classmates; the team views this as a secondary function.

Selection and Development of Behavior Change Tool(s)

☒ Reinforcement-Based Tools

Terri and Mr. Denst will create a reinforcement menu using Terri's responses to the Behavior Interview and Reinforcement Survey. Mr. Denst will use the Reinforcement Survey as a discussion-starter. Mr. Denst, Ms. Williams, Terri's parents, and Terri will develop and sign a contingency contract for Terri's use of her new skills. She will learn those new skills as part of the skill-based tool intervention. Both school and home rewards will be included. The reinforcement-based tool intervention will be initiated once the skill-based tool intervention is in place. Mr. Denst will inform the team when to initiate the reinforcement-based tool intervention (when he and Terri believe she has mastered her new skills to a level where application in the classroom setting can be reasonably expected). Ms. Williams will monitor Terri's use of her new skills, and will execute the contingency contract. She will communicate with Mrs. Logan so the home portion of the contract is executed.

☒ Belief-Based Tools

The team wants to address Terri's disabling belief that she is not as smart as her classmates. Ms. Van and Ms. Williams will present Terri's achievement profile to Terri and her parents (obviously in terms a third grader can understand). The team feels that Terri's failure to acquire reading skill is primarily due to inappropriate and inconsistent instruction. Terri has many areas of strength, including her mastery of mathematical facts and concepts—these will be stressed. Ms. Williams will begin a process of reviewing Terri's assignments and work production with Terri. Terri needs to see the quality and quantity of the good work she does.

X Skill-Based Tools

Mr. Denst will work with Terri to help her identify triggers and develop internal controls and socially appropriate emotional drain-off techniques. Mr. Denst will use "Skillstreaming the Elementary School Child: A Guide for Teaching Prosocial Skills" and "Relaxation: A Comprehensive Manual." The team identified the following specific skills from "Skillstreaming": Using Self Control (#26), Dealing With Embarrassment (#34), and Deciding on Your Abilities (#46). Mr. Denst and Terri will meet 1 day a week during Terri's physical education class period. The team feels Terri will acquire the necessary skills quickly and that her motivation will ensure her success. The team estimates that four to five training sessions will be needed.

X Needs-Based Tools

The parents and the rest of the team feel Terri needs to feel competent. Mr. and Mrs. Logan have decided to enroll Terri in an age-group gymnastics class. Once Terri progresses, she will be able to participate in competitions. Her parents believe she will do quite well, and think it will give her something to be proud of. Terri's brother and sister do not participate in gymnastics, so there will be no sibling rivalry. School personnel believe this is a wonderful idea, and will support it by talking with Terri about her involvement. They will also attend competitions when appropriate.

X Environment-Based Tools

With Terri's permission, Terri's classmates will be informed of Terri's Plan to Do Better. They will be asked not to respond to any silly comments Terri may make while she is trying to change her behavior. With the help of Mrs. Smith, Ms. Williams will make accommodations for Terri during reading instruction and related activities. Ms. Williams will also read an article on accommodations and one on tiered lessons, and will meet with Mrs. Smith to discuss how they can work together to delineate the roles each will play in providing a meaningful intervention for Terri. Terri will also receive an intensive remedial reading intervention provided by Mrs. Smith, which will take place during Terri's normal physical education class. This intervention is scheduled for a 3-month period, 4 days a week. This intervention will be changed to 5 days a week once Terri no longer needs to work with Mr. Denst for the implementation of the skill-based intervention. The team feels Terri's work with Mr. Denst will take a short period of time (around a month). Mr. Denst will keep the team apprised of Terri's progress so that a decision can be made regarding the increase from 4 to 5 days.

Description of the Behavior Change Plan's Assessment (Process and Schedule)

Mr. Todd will review the plan with the team to make sure everyone is on the same page. This is important, as several individuals are involved in implementation and assessment. Mr. Denst has agreed to host a 20-minute update meeting in his office on the second Thursday of the month during communications period (plan time). Attendance is mandatory for Ms. Williams, Mrs. Smith, and Mr. Denst. All other team members are welcome (parents have a standing invitation). Ms. Williams and Mrs. Smith will assess Terri's progress in the remedial reading program and classroom instruction on a weekly basis. Mr. Denst will let Ms. Williams know when Terri is ready for the contingency contract to be initiated. Terri's performance on her contingency contract will be tracked by Ms. Williams. Ms. Williams will continue to provide Terri evidence of her academic competency, and she will monitor Terri's belief concerning her competency. Ms. Williams will keep abreast of Terri's gymnastic participation so she can discuss Terri's accomplishments with her on a regular basis.

Other Notes

Terri is physically fit and performs well in physical education class. She will be participating in a gymnastics program outside of school, and the team believes she can miss physical education for a 3-month period. Mr. and Mrs. Logan have given their written permission for this schedule adjustment. Terri was not referred for a special education comprehensive case study. She will receive intensive services from Mrs. Smith, the special education resource teacher, for a period of 3 months. At the end of the intervention, Terri's performance will be reevaluated. The team believes the Plan to Do Better will not result in a referral to special education. Terri's parents are very supportive of the plan and also hope to avoid a referral for special education services. Ms. Williams and Mrs. Smith will be using "Adapting Curriculum and Instruction in Inclusive Classrooms: A Teacher's Desk Reference." The behavior change team will purchase a copy for Ms. Williams.

Essential Questions Summary for Terri

The team used the following information-gathering tools from the previous chapter:

- ※ Parent or Guardian Survey (page 56)
- ※ Behavior Interview and Reinforcement Survey (page 59)
- ※ This Is Me (page 73)
- ※ I Prefer to Learn (page 75)

Terri is conscious of the behavior: She said she feels like everyone is looking at her prior to her blurting things out. She did not realize that the behavior almost exclusively occurs during reading instruction and related activities. The team is not really sure if Terri is in control of the behavior; it seems she just reacts. Terri understands that her behavior is a problem, and not something she is supposed to do.

Terri could predict the reactions of her classmates and teacher. However, she was not aware of how disruptive her speaking out had become to her learning and that of her classmates. Terri has a significant need to fit in, not to stand out. She very much wants to be accepted by her classmates and to please her teacher and parents. Terri believes she is not as smart as her classmates and siblings. She knows that she struggles in reading (and has for some time). She does not realize that she has good learning potential and some real academic strengths.

A review of Terri's school records and present performance indicates that the previous and current instructional program failed to meet Terri's learning needs. The environment appears to be putting Terri in a difficult position, especially in relation to her competency belief and need to be accepted. It was also worthy to note that Terri's classmates may be reinforcing her outbursts with their attention. When Terri feels her lack of reading skills may lead to embarrassment, the behavior definitely helps her to avoid the awkwardness.

Terri does not possess the academic skills necessary to actively participate in or benefit from the reading program. In addition, she does not employ a socially acceptable method for handling the pressure this causes. The team felt Terri's behavior was a reasonable reaction to the situation, especially considering the limited experience and coping mechanisms typical for a girl her age.

Several team members identified Terri's candor and attitude as specific strengths. The entire team believes Terri will welcome the behavior change plan. The information Mr. and Mrs. Logan provided—about Terri's struggles in her previous school and her relationship with her siblings—was very helpful. The parents and their participation in the plan are another reason to feel encouraged. The team especially liked the parents' idea of involving Terri in an age-group gymnastics program, as it will give Terri something to feel good about.

Resources Used for Terri

- Cautela, J., & Groden, J. (1978). *Relaxation: A comprehensive manual for adults, children, and children with special needs.* Champaign, IL: Research Press Company.

- Deschenes, C., Ebeling, D., & Sprague, T. (1994). *Adapting curriculum and instruction in inclusive classrooms: A teacher's desk reference.* Bloomington, IN: Institute for the Study of Developmental Disabilities.

- McGinnis, E., Goldstein, A., Sprafkin, R. P., & Gershaw, N. J. (1984). *Skillstreaming the elementary school child: A guide for teaching prosocial skills.* Champaign, IL: Research Press Company.

Plan to Do Better

Student _Jarrel Smith_ **Grade** _6th_ **School/Program/Class** _General education_

Team Members

Mr. Pitt, classroom teacher

Mrs. Gills, classroom teacher

Mrs. Armela, classroom teacher and team leader

Mr. Hollis, assistant principal

Mr. Bult, custodian

Ms. Martel, social worker

Jarrel Smith, student

Mr. and Mrs. Smith, parents

Date Initiated _2/3/06_   **Date Reviewed** _____

· ·

Description of Nonproductive Behavior, Including the Behavior's Specific Characteristics and Context

Jarrel becomes verbally or physically aggressive with peers when he perceives he is being challenged. The behavior occurs in all settings, at any time of day. Examples of his verbal aggression are, "Who are you looking at? Do you want something, punk? I'll smack you right here." With regard to physical aggression, Jarrel gets within inches of the student he is targeting, pushes, muffs (soft, open-handed blows to the back of the head), and engages in a full-blown fight if the targeted student does not back down. In most instances, staff members have intervened prior to a fight occurring. Jarrel accepts direction from staff members; while he may mutter something under his breath, he does not respond to staff members in a verbally or physically aggressive manner. Consequences for the behavior have included students backing down, students responding in kind, verbal directives from teachers, removal from class, after-school detentions, external suspensions, and parent conferences.

View, Input, and Suggestions of the Student (Required) and Parents or Significant Adults (Recommended)

Mrs. Smith completed the Parent or Guardian Survey. Mrs. Smith and Jarrel were active participants in the team meeting to develop the Plan to Do Better. Jarrel said, "I don't start stuff, I just don't let myself be punked out [disrespected]. I can tell when someone is getting ready to front me [embarrass me in front of peers]. I keep it real; this is how it is where I come from." Mrs. Smith said, "We live in a pretty tough area. Jarrel has learned not to let his guard down. My husband tells Jarrel not to start stuff, but to take care of his business so that people know they can't push him around. I try to explain to my husband that it doesn't work like that in school. It gets Jarrel in trouble."

Description of the Function(s) of the Behavior

Jarrel is not a bully or a gang member. He does not use his physical prowess to get things or to enforce his will on his classmates. The team believes the problem behavior functions to get the respect of his classmates, avoid being the target of his classmates, and earn his father's approval.

Selection and Development of Behavior Change Tool(s)

☒ Reinforcement-Based Tools

Mr. Pitt and Jarrel designed the reinforcement-based intervention. All teachers and staff will be made aware of the Plan to Do Better, including the new skills learned through the skill-based intervention (see the section on skill-based tools later in this plan). Teachers and staff will record and report to Mrs. Armela (team leader) anytime they observe Jarrel using his new skills. Jarrel will log whenever he uses his new skills and report to Mrs. Armela (the log will be inserted in his assignment book). After five uses of new skills, Jarrel can choose from the reinforcement menu he and Mr. Pitt developed. Every time Jarrel is able to access the reinforcement menu, a home report will be sent home. The reinforcement-based intervention will not be activated until belief-based, skill-based, and environment-based interventions are in place.

☒ Belief-Based Tools

The Smiths will participate in a 6-hour anger management parent and student workshop provided by the district's Safe and Secure School Team. The workshop addresses Mr. Smith's and Jarrel's beliefs that a man must handle challenges with verbal or physical aggression. The workshop also offers socially acceptable strategies and skills for handling anger. The Smiths accepted the school's suggestion to try to find a way to avoid the need for repeated negative consequences (such as detentions and suspensions). Ms. Martel (social worker) and Mr. Bult (custodian) will watch the movie "A Bronx Tale" (DeNiro [Director/Producer], 1993) with Jarrel (the team used the www.teachwithmovies.org website to help them find an appropriate movie). Then Mr. Bult will discuss with Jarrel how a man handles challenges. They will also discuss what it means to be a man. Jarrel will help Mr. Bult care for and maintain the school's 50-gallon aquarium. Jarrel expressed a desire to learn about tropical fish, and Mr. Bult is an expert. Mr. Bult will not only talk with Jarrel about fish, he will talk with him about his Plan to Do Better. The team believes Mr. Bult will be a wonderful role model for Jarrel. Their common interest will provide a way for them to spend time together and serve as a catalyst for the formation of their relationship.

☒ Skill-Based Tools

Jarrel will receive specific skills training to allow him to avoid challenges and fights without losing face. Ms. Martel will work one-on-one 2 days a week with Jarrel during homeroom using the appropriate skills from "Skillstreaming the Adolescent." Ms. Martel will begin with Standing Up for Your Rights (#27), Avoiding Trouble With Others (#29), and Keeping Out of Fights (#30). She will also use scenarios from "Ready-to-Use Conflict Resolution Activities for Secondary Students" to help Jarrel with situational perception.

☒ Needs-Based Tools

While a needs-based intervention will not be part of the initial plan, team members (especially Mr. Pitt, Mr. Bult, and Ms. Martel) will engage Jarrel in conversation regarding his lack of friends at school. At some point, with Jarrel's approval, a needs-based intervention may be developed to help Jarrel form some real friendships.

☒ Environment-Based Tools

All teachers and staff will be made aware of Jarrel's Plan to Do Better and will cue the use of the substitute behavior by addressing Jarrel as Mr. Smith. Mr. Smith will be used as a signal to Jarrel to immediately use his new skills.

Description of the Behavior Change Plan's Assessment (Process and Schedule)

The skill-based tool will be assessed on a weekly basis through a review of staff and student logs. Jarrel's entire plan will be reviewed at the weekly grade-level team meeting. In addition to the log review, the team will review Jarrel's standard discipline record. Mr. Bult will attend the grade-level team meeting to report on his time with Jarrel in the belief-based tool intervention. The behavior change team thinks Mr. Bult may be the first person to observe changes in Jarrel's belief system (such as what it means to be a man). Mrs. Armela will call home on a weekly basis to discuss the grade-level team's weekly review with Jarrel's parents.

Other Notes

The written plan will be reviewed by Mrs. Armela (grade-level team leader) with Jarrel and his parents, the grade-level team, and the school's discipline team. Mr. Hollis (assistant principal) will present highlights to general staff. The Smiths (including Jarrel) view the plan as a good faith attempt to help Jarrel stay in class and in school. It will be very important to keep Jarrel's parents in the loop, in order to make sure communication with Jarrel's parents is accurate and purposeful. All communications will funnel through Mrs. Armela (this includes any standard *disciplinary actions taken by the school's discipline team). The team wants to protect the emerging positive school-family relationship. Ms. Martel decided to use the high school conflict resolution resource instead of the adolescent level, believing that Jarrel would find the scenarios and role-plays more realistic.*

Essential Questions Summary for Jarrel

The problem-solving team felt that Mr. Pitt and Mrs. Gills had offered a more-than-adequate definition of the nonproductive behavior, including the behavior's characteristics and context. The team conducted a review of Jarrel's academic record (which showed an average student who works hard and performs well) and his discipline record (which indicated frequent referrals out of class, several after-school detentions, four external suspensions, and three parent conferences). All his classroom teachers reviewed their plan books to establish the frequency of the behavior and to consider any effect it might be having on Jarrel's academic performance. They determined that Jarrel's behavior has a negative effect on his skill acquisition and academic performance. His time out of class, both in the office and in external suspension, limits his exposure to the curriculum, and Jarrel has not always made up missed assignments.

Jarrel selected Mr. Pitt to interview him. Mr. Pitt investigated Jarrel's insights into the behavior and its function. Mr. Pitt used the following forms:

- ⅏ Behavior Interview and Reinforcement Survey (page 59)
- ⅏ Things My Teacher Should Know About Me—Interest Inventory for Middle School Students (page 65)

Since Mr. Pitt is Jarrel's favorite teacher, the team wanted Mr. Pitt to engage Jarrel not only in a discussion specifically related to the problematic behavior, but also in a discussion that would help Jarrel relax, drop his guard, and become part of the team instead of viewing himself as something the team was supposed to work on or fix. Jarrel reported that he is "okay" with school and that he has lots of acquaintances in school, but not a lot of close friends. He said his real friends are the friends he hangs with outside of school. He likes to play basketball, but not enough to try out for the school team. He really enjoys time spent with his mom, dad, and siblings. He also volunteered that he likes the adults at school (especially the "cool ones," Mr. Pitt and Mr. Hollis).

The team believes Jarrel is conscious of the behavior; however, Jarrel is hypervigilant and is easily engaged emotionally. His reaction to a perceived challenge is automatic at this point (little—if any—thinking occurs). Jarrel has some control over the behavior based on his processing ability and his acceptance of adult direction. However, he does not think before reacting to what he perceives to be a challenge by a classmate; instead, he simply reacts to the classmate. Jarrel's interview included a review of rules and expectations. Jarrel indicated that he knows what is expected of him in school. There is definitely some confusion between school expectations and his father's (and possibly his community's)

expectations. Jarrel could not articulate the long-term consequences of his behavior. He was able to explain what happens as immediate responses to the behavior (both classmate and adult responses).

The team believes Jarrel has a strong need to control his environment and to be perceived as an individual who does what is necessary to maintain control. He absolutely equates "being a man" with being willing and able to handle challenges with verbal or physical aggression. This belief is confirmed regularly by his father.

Peer reaction is reinforcing the behavior for the most part. Teachers and school personnel are punishing the behavior without achieving the desired result. Parental responses are mixed; however, Mr. Smith is definitely reinforcing the behavior.

The team believes that Jarrel does not possess the skill set required for him to respond to challenges in a productive, more socially acceptable manner. Jarrel has not had appropriate role models. In fact, he has most likely had inappropriate counterproductive role models. The team believes the school's custodian can be a productive role model based on his temperament, his reputation with the kids, and the interest in tropical fish he and Jarrel share.

The behavior allows Jarrel to get what he considers to be respect from his peers. It also conforms to the definition of what a man is, as conveyed by his father; it allows Jarrel to enjoy his father's acceptance and approval. The behavior also protects Jarrel from becoming a target for aggressive peers.

Resources Used for Jarrel

※ DeNiro, R. (Director/Producer). (1993). *A Bronx tale* [Motion picture]. United States: B. T. Films, Inc.

※ Goldstein, A. P., Sprafkin, R. P., Gershaw, N. J., & Klein, P. (1980). *Skillstreaming the adolescent.* Champaign, IL: Research Press Company.

※ Perlstein, R., & Thrall, G. (1996). *Ready-to-use conflict resolution activities for secondary students.* Paramus, NJ: Center for Applied Research in Education.

Plan to Do Better

Student _Tommy Krakow_   **Grade** _8th_   **School/Program/Class** _Special education,_
                                                           behavior-disordered

Team Members

Mr. Morales, classroom teacher

Mrs. Monroe, teacher's aide

Mrs. Thomas, social worker and therapist

Mr. Passano, behavior intervention specialist

Tommy Krakow, student

Mrs. Krakow, parent

Date Initiated _10/10/05_   **Date Reviewed** _____

. . . .

Description of Nonproductive Behavior, Including the Behavior's Specific Characteristics and Context

Tommy bullies classmates who are weaker (either physically or psychologically). The bullying
occurs out of the direct supervision of adults. It takes the form of comments that make the targeted
student feel stupid, inadequate, or ostracized. It is also demonstrated by verbal intimidation and
physical actions (arm-twisting, hard pinching, pushing, and punching). The behavior can occur in
the classroom, but it occurs more often during recess and lunch, or in the hallway.

View, Input, and Suggestions of the Student (Required) and Parents or Significant Adults (Recommended)

Tommy does not acknowledge his bullying behavior, nor does he see himself as a bully. He sees the
students he bullies as "babies who make a mountain out of a mole hill." Mr. and Mrs. Krakow
believe Tommy when he tells them the other kids are making things up to get him in trouble. They
were reluctant to participate in the Plan to Do Better process, but ultimately did so.

Description of the Function(s) of the Behavior

The behavior's function is to allow Tommy to get what he wants and control the outcomes of his
interactions with his classmates. Tommy holds some disabling beliefs, and his behavior is an
extension of these beliefs. He believes that his wants supersede those of others and that he should
always win and get his way.

Selection and Development of Behavior Change Tool(s)

✗ Reinforcement-Based Tools

Tommy is one of the strongest academic performers in his class. After the belief-based

interventions begin to take hold, Tommy will be recruited by Mr. Morales to be a peer tutor. Mr. Morales was hesitant in the past to assign Tommy a peer tutor role, because most students would have rejected Tommy's help. Mr. Morales thinks that once Tommy begins to develop some empathy, this role will serve as reinforcement.

Belief-Based Tools

Tommy identified Mrs. Monroe as someone he trusts. Mrs. Monroe will present Tommy the results of the lunchroom and playground observations that confirm his bullying behavior. She will attempt to get Tommy to accept the results. Tommy and Mrs. Monroe will read the article "Remembering Brian," a mother's account of how bullying drove her son to commit suicide. Tommy will also select two readings from the school's Character Education Literature List (one from the Caring section and one from the Respect section), and the readings will be discussed to help Tommy acknowledge and process his bullying behavior. Discussions will focus on the effects of bullying on the victim and the bully. They will also explore the difference between being feared and respected.

Skill-Based Tools

Tommy will work individually with Mrs. Thomas on developing more appropriate interaction skills. With Tommy's help, Mrs. Thomas will pick and choose from "The Bully, the Bullied, and Beyond." Mrs. Thomas will recruit a caring classmate or two to help Tommy practice emerging interaction skills. Mrs. Thomas will teach a unit on bullying to Tommy's class. Lessons will include strategies for victims and bystanders. Tommy's classmates will be empowered to respond effectively to bullying. Lessons will be selected and adapted from "Bully-Proofing Your School."

Needs-Based Tools

Tommy's classmates will be challenged to make sure that Tommy is welcomed and included in all activities. The goal is to address Tommy's need to be included. Materials from "Bully-Proofing Your School" will be used to empower Tommy's classmates to move from being a "silent majority" to a "caring majority."

Environment-Based Tools

Tommy's parents and Tommy have agreed that Tommy's Plan to Do Better will be shared with his classmates prior to its implementation (Tommy was reluctant, but the encouragement of school personnel and his parents prevailed). Tommy will be given a "hero contingency contract" that stipulates a classroom reward whenever Tommy banks 5 days without a bullying incident.

Description of the Behavior Change Plan's Assessment (Process and Schedule)

Mr. Morales and Mrs. Monroe will work closely with Mrs. Thomas to implement and assess the plan. Mr. Morales will assess the plan on a weekly basis; he will need to receive regular reports *from the lunchroom and recess supervisors. Mr. Morales, Mrs. Monroe, and Mrs. Thomas have agreed to review Tommy's plan at their weekly clinical team meetings. Tommy has agreed that his plan will be reviewed as part of the weekly classroom meeting with his peers. Mr. Morales will ask for input from Tommy's classmates and encourage student-to-student dialogue. Mrs. Thomas will participate in the classroom meeting to help Tommy "find his place" in the classroom and to gain insight she can use in her individual work with Tommy.*

Other Notes

Tommy's classmates will be encouraged to help Tommy change his behavior; they are viewed as an integral part of the plan. Mr. Morales will include an update on Tommy's Plan to Do Better in the progress note he sends home every Friday.

Essential Questions Summary for Tommy

In addition to a review of school records, the problem-solving team used the following forms:

- Student Interview Form (page 55)
- Parent or Guardian Survey (page 56)
- Things My Teacher Should Know About Me: Interest Inventory for Middle School Students (page 65)
- Teachers Who Help Me Succeed (page 76)

The Student Interview Form was used to interview Tommy and four classmates. It was interesting to note that while Tommy did not acknowledge the bullying behavior, all four of his classmates did. One of Tommy's classmates was very helpful and shared an insight that he "thought Tommy really wanted to be part of the group." His classmates' responses verified that unless Tommy imposes himself into the group, he is often left out (primarily due to Tommy's abrasive behavior). Tommy's classmates painted a picture of an individual who believes he should always get his way. The team has seen this same disabling belief in other students who bully.

Tommy has a negative view of school and his special education placement. He does feel his teacher and aide are nice to him and want to see him do well. Responses from Tommy and his parents indicate that Tommy has few friends at school; while he has a few friends he plays with in the community, these are children 2 to 3 years younger. Much of his free time at home is spent watching television, playing video games, and exploring the Internet. The team believes Tommy does not possess age-appropriate social skills for interaction.

The environment is maintaining the behavior. The behavior has allowed Tommy to get something to enforce his will, get his way, win, and feel powerful. A review of the classroom behavior management system revealed that negative consequences that are part of the system have seldom been imposed, since the behavior has occurred outside of adult observation. The team conducted observations of Tommy at lunch and recess, and confirmed the bullying behavior Tommy's classmates had been reporting. These observations were important; not only did they establish that Tommy was bullying, but they also provided evidence and new information to be used to facilitate Tommy making a belief change. They also helped Tommy's parents accept the fact that Tommy was bullying.

Resources Used for Tommy

- Head, R. (1996, Spring). Remembering Brian. *Reclaiming Children and Youth,* *5*(1), 6-9.

- Garrity, C., Jens, K., Porter, W., Sager, N., & Short-Camilli, C. (2004). *Bully-proofing your school.* Longmont, CO: Sopris West.

- Williams, E. (2005). *The bully, the bullied and beyond.* Chapin, SC: YouthLight, Inc.

Plan to Do Better

Student   Nick Ramano   **Grade** 10th   **School/Program/Class**   *General education,*
college preparation

Team Members

Mr. Sanfrentello, English teacher and hockey coach

Mr. Snow, math teacher

Mr. Hull, dean

Mr. McKenzie, psychologist

Nick Ramano, student

Mr. and Mrs. Ramano, parents

Date Initiated   11/10/04   **Date Reviewed** _____

• •

Description of Nonproductive Behavior, Including the Behavior's Specific Characteristics and Context

Nick is verbally inappropriate and disrespectful to adults. He will tell adults to "get off" him, to leave him alone, and that he can do what he wants. Nick does not swear; he will raise his voice and show an angry face. The behavior occurs in all settings when an adult attempts to redirect or limit Nick's actions.

View, Input, and Suggestions of the Student (Required) and Parents or Significant Adults (Recommended)

Information from Nick's survey revealed several areas of interest including hockey, hanging out with his friends, and camping with his dad. It also showed that he works after school at a florist and is responsible for babysitting his younger siblings during the week and on the weekends. Nick said that he feels he is not particularly smart and that by the time a guy is in high school, he should be able to figure things out without the help of adults. He said his dad wants him to try out for a junior league (semiprofessional) hockey team this year. Nick believes that good hockey players have to be aggressive and defend themselves when confronted. Nick's mom filled out the Parent Survey, and both parents were interviewed over the phone. Both parents work full-time jobs and supplement them with second jobs. Nick's mom feels that her husband puts too much emphasis on sports. She feels that Nick is exhausted from working, playing hockey, and babysitting, and is too tired when he should spend more time doing homework and studying. When asked about Nick, his dad said, "He's a real smart kid who is sort of lazy and not motivated." He also stated that there

is a lot of tension in the home due to financial problems. He said he and his wife have full-time and part-time jobs, leaving little time for fun and family activities. Mrs. Ramano, Mr. Ramano, and Nick participated in the team meeting (Mr. Ramano by phone) to develop the Plan to Do Better.

Description of the Function(s) of the Behavior

Nick's behavior serves the dual function of allowing him to stay true to his beliefs (he does not require any help, nor should he have to submit to adult direction) and getting him adult attention (interaction).

Selection and Development of Behavior Change Tool(s)

☐ Reinforcement-Based Tools

_____

_____

_____

☒ Belief-Based Tools

Nick will watch the movie "The Miracle" (about the 1980 United States Olympic hockey team's defeat of Russia) with his coach. Nick and his coach will discuss the different players, identify their struggles, discuss their beliefs, and identify their problem-solving styles (especially within the context of the coach's style). They will identify positive characteristics of specific players and their methods for dealing with frustration and situational realities. Nick will choose one of his teachers with whom to watch the movie "White Squall." They will then discuss the need for rules and the need for legitimate authority to be respected. Nick will meet with his coach and a school counselor to review college admissions requirements and athletic scholarship opportunities. The counselor will review Nick's performance on standardized tests to highlight his potential and offer evidence of just how smart he really is. The counselor will also present a comparison of earning potential and lifestyle potential of high school graduates and college graduates.

☒ Skill-Based Tools

Mr. McKenzie will meet with Nick for time management instruction. Mr. McKenzie will use selected material from "The 7 Habits of Highly Effective Teens," as well as other materials. A color-coding system will be employed for helping Nick to use the school calendar, his practice and game schedule, his assignment book, and his work schedule when organizing his time. A master calendar will also be developed.

☒ Needs-Based Tools

Nick and his father have decided to spend some time every week alone together. Due to their other commitments, they will meet Sunday evening to choose the activity and the time for the upcoming week.

☒ Environment-Based Tools

All Nick's teachers will provide Nick a verbal cue indicating that he must accept their request immediately. The agreed-upon cue is for the teacher to refer to Nick as Nicholas. Nick felt this cue would be helpful, and he appreciated the discrete nature of the intervention. As Nick put it, "It is a real nice personal way to tell me to shut up."

Description of the Behavior Change Plan's Assessment (Process and Schedule)

Mr. Hull will monitor the plan through a weekly progress report that all of Nick's teachers will complete. The report includes both a behavioral and an academic assessment. The report also requires the teachers to include a brief narrative describing Nick's attitude and demeanor. Mr. Hull and Nick will meet every Monday during Nick's study hall period to review Nick's progress. Mr. Hull and Nick will determine if they need to invite anyone else to the Monday meeting. Mr. Hull will touch base with Nick's parents at least twice a month (via a note or a phone call).

Other Notes

Nick's parents have decided that they will find a way to reduce the time Nick spends caring for his siblings. Rather than developing a specific reinforcement-based tool, the team and Nick reviewed the likely possibility that left unaddressed, the problem behavior will interfere with his eligibility to play hockey. Nick was a contributing member of the behavior change plan team. He did a good job of completing the Student Interview Form and participating in team meetings. Consideration was given to shortening Nick's school day. Options for doing so for the next semester included the elimination of study hall and some form of participation in the Cooperative Work Study (CWS) program.

Essential Questions Summary for Nick

Mr. and Mrs. Ramano completed the Parent or Guardian Survey. The survey was reviewed, and subsequent phone interviews were conducted with both parents. The team's information-gathering included the following:

- The dean's review of Nick's discipline record showed 18 referrals to the dean so far this year, most for falling asleep in class, refusal to follow directions, and disrespect.

- Academic progress reports showed that Nick is passing all his classes (five Cs), but seriously underperforming. All teachers indicated he was missing assignments and homework.

- Standardized tests indicated Nick's performance is in the 90th percentile across subjects.

※ A statement submitted by Nick's hockey coach said Nick is a talented and enthusiastic player who gives 100% during practice and games, but is repeatedly late to practice. The team practices 3 nights a week for 90 minutes and has a 50-game schedule.

Nick is a very active young man. His interests include hockey, spending time with friends, and camping with his Dad. Nick has a part-time job at a local florist and is responsible for babysitting his younger siblings approximately 15 hours a week. Nick does not particularly like school. He knows he must maintain academic eligibility to play hockey, and he does just enough to do so.

Nick is conscious of the problem behavior. He knows what he does and believes his actions are justified and reasonable. The team believes the behavior is under Nick's control. Nick indicated that he could stop if he wanted to. Nick understands the school's code of conduct, but cannot see why the adults at school should be able to tell him what to do. Nick seems to have little understanding of how his actions affect other people, his relationships with them, and his education and future prospects. He did acknowledge that the problem behavior had led to detentions, internal suspensions, and one external suspension.

The team believes there is a connection between Nick's need for adult attention and his behavior. There is a significant relationship between Nick's beliefs and his behavior. He believes he has all the rights adults have; he does not recognize their legitimate authority. He operates with a great deal of independence at home and acts as an adult when he cares for his younger siblings. He believes he should be treated as an adult in school and should be able to make his own decisions without adult involvement.

The school environment is designed to change behavior by applying positive and negative consequences; these consequences have not been successful in changing the behavior. Nick is not invested in his education other than maintaining eligibility to play hockey. The environment has no meaningful rewards or punishments to apply. The team (with Nick's participation) considered making Nick's participation on the hockey team contingent upon Nick correcting his behavior. The team decided that hockey was a very positive and important force in Nick's life, and it chose not to attempt to design a reinforcement-based behavior change intervention involving hockey. Instead, the team discussed how the problem behavior could affect Nick's eligibility if it continues. If the behavior continues, it is likely that the number of external suspensions will increase, and the school's code of conduct prohibits interscholastic competition while serving suspension. External suspension usually has an effect on grades, and this was pointed out. These rules will be applied to Nick as with any other student.

The team was sure Nick had the necessary skills to allow him to interact appropriately with adults at school. The team did think Nick might lack some executive skills, and considering the pace of Nick's life, this could cause undue stress. Nick seems to have bad days. A review of Nick's discipline record confirmed that the problem behavior occurred multiple times during a single day. Nick had 1 or 2 bad days a week. The team hypothesized these were days when Nick was stressed out.

Resources Used for Nick

- Ciardi, M. (Producer), & O'Connor, G. (Director). (2004). *The miracle* [Motion picture]. United States: Pop Pop Productions.
- Covey, S. (1998). *The 7 habits of highly effective teens*. New York: Simon & Schuster.
- Gitlin, M. (Producer), & Scott, R. (Director). (1996). *White squall* [Motion picture]. United States: Hollywood Pictures.

References and Resources

Bandura, A. (1974). Behavior theory and the models of man. *American Psychologist, 29,* 859–869.

Bandura, A. (1977). Self-efficacy: Toward a unifying theory of behavioral change. *Psychological Review, 84,* 191–215.

Batsche, G., Elliot, J., Graden, J. L., Grimes, J., Kovaleski, J. E., Prasse, D., Reschly, D. J., Schrag, J., & Tilly III, W. D. (2005). *Response to intervention: Policy considerations and implementation.* Alexandria, VA: National Association of State Directors of Special Education.

Cautela, J., & Groden, J. (1978). *Relaxation: A comprehensive manual for adults, children and children with special needs.* Champaign, IL: Research Press Company.

Ciardi, M. (Producer), & O'Connor, G. (Director). (2004). *The miracle* [Motion picture]. United States: Pop Pop Productions.

Coles, S., Horvath, B., Chapman, C., Deschenes, C., Ebeling, D., & Sprague, J. (2000). *Adapting curriculum and instruction in inclusive classrooms: A teacher's desk reference.* Bloomington, IN: Indiana University Center for Excellence in Developmental Disabilities.

Conroy, M. A., Clark, D., Gable, R. A., & Fox, J. J. (1999). A look at IDEA 1997 Discipline Provisions: Implications for changes in the roles and responsibilities of school personnel. *Preventing School Failure, 43*(2), 64–70.

Conroy, M. A., Clark, D., Katsiyannis, A., Gable, R., & Fox, J. (2000, November). *The IDEAS 97 Disciplinary Provisions: National Trends and State Policies and Practices.* Paper presented at 24th Annual Conference on Severe Behavior Disorders of Children and Youth, Scottsdale, AZ.

Covey, S. (1989). *The 7 habits of highly effective people.* New York: Simon & Schuster.

Covey, S. (1997). *The 7 habits of highly effective families.* New York: Golden Books.

Covey, S. (1998). *The 7 habits of highly effective teens.* New York: Simon & Schuster.

Curwin, R., & Mendler, A. (1988, 1999). *Discipline with dignity.* Alexandria, VA: Association for Supervision and Curriculum Development.

DeNiro, R. (Director/Producer). (1993). *A Bronx tale* [Motion picture]. United States: B. T. Films, Inc.

Deschenes, C., Ebeling, D., & Sprague, T. (1994). *Adapting curriculum and instruction in inclusive classrooms: A teacher's desk reference.* Bloomington, IN: Institute for the Study of Developmental Disabilities.

Division for Learning Disabilities. (2007). *Thinking about response to intervention and learning disabilities: A teacher's guide.* Arlington, VA: Author.

Dunlap, G. (1993). Functional analysis of classroom variables for students with emotional and behavioral disorders. *Behavioral Disorders, 18*(4), 275–291.

Frank, L. S., & Panico, A. (2000, 2007). *Adventure education for the classroom community: Over 90 activities for developing character, responsibility, and the courage to achieve.* Bloomington, IN: Solution Tree (formerly National Educational Service).

Gable, R. A., & Hendrickson, J. M. (2000). Strategies for maintaining positive behavior change stemming from functional behavioral assessment in schools. *Education and Treatment of Children, 23*(3), 286–295.

Gable, R. A., Hendrickson, J. M., & Smith, C. J. (1999). Changing discipline policies and practices: Finding a place for functional behavioral assessment in schools. *Preventing School Failure, 43*(4), 167–170.

Gable, R. A., Hendrickson, J. M., Tonelson, S. W., & Van Acker, R. (2002, August). Integrating academic and non-academic instruction for students with emotional/behavioral disorders. *Education and Treatment of Children, 25*(3), 459–475.

Gable, R. A., Quinn, M. M., Rutherford, R. B. Jr., Howell, K. W., & Hoffman, C. C. (2000). *Addressing student problem behavior—Part III: Creating positive behavioral intervention plans and supports.* Washington, DC: Center for Effective Collaboration and Practice.

Garrity, C., Jens, K., Porter, W., Sager, N., & Short-Camilli, C. (2004). *Bully-proofing your school.* Longmont, CO: Sopris West.

Gitlin, M. (Producer), & Scott, R. (Director). (1996). *White squall* [Motion picture]. United States: Hollywood Pictures.

Glasser, W. (1996). *Schools without failure.* New York: Harper & Row.

Glasser, W. (2001). *Choice theory in the classroom.* New York: Harper.

Goldstein, A. P., Sprafkin, R. P., Gershaw, N. J., & Klein, P. (1980). *Skillstreaming the adolescent.* Champaign, IL: Research Press Company.

Greene, R. W., & Ablon, J. S. (2006). *Treating explosive kids: The collaborative problem solving approach.* New York: Guilford Press.

Head, R. (1996, Spring). Remembering Brian. *Reclaiming Children and Youth, 5*(1), 6–9.

Hendrickson, J., Gable, R., Conroy, M., Fox, J., & Smith, C. (1999, August). Behavioral problems in schools: Ways to encourage functional behavioral assessment (FBA) of discipline-evoking behavior of students with emotional and/or behavioral disorders (EBD). *Education and Treatment of Children, 22*(3), 280–290.

Howell, K., & Nelson, K. (1999, August). Has public policy exceeded our knowledge base? This is a two-part question. *Behavioral Disorders, 24*(4), 331–334.

Individuals with Disabilities Education Act (IDEA). (1997). *Federal Register 71*(156).

Individuals with Disabilities Education Improvement Act (IDEIA). 20 U. S. C. Sec. 1400 (2004).

Jones, F. (2000). *Tools for teaching.* Santa Cruz, CA: Fredric H. Jones & Associates, Inc.

Kaplan, J. S. (2000). *Beyond functional assessment: A social-cognitive approach to the evaluation of behavior problems in children and youth.* Austin, TX: PRO-ED.

Kaplan, J. S., & Carter, J. (1995). *Beyond behavior and modification.* Austin, TX: PRO-ED.

Kohn, A. (1993). *Punished by rewards.* Boston: Houghton Mifflin.

Lickona, T. (1992). *Educating for character.* New York: Bantam Books.

McCall, N. (1995). *Makes me wanna holler: A young black man in America.* New York: Vintage Books.

McGinnis, E., Goldstein, A., Sprafkin, R. P., & Gershaw, N. J. (1984). *Skillstreaming the elementary school child: A guide for teaching prosocial skills.* Champaign IL: Research Press Company.

Nelson, C. M. (1998, September). *Multi-component interventions for prevention and effective practice.* Paper presented at the U.S. Department of Education's IDEA Institute on Discipline Provisions, Kansas City, MO.

Nelson, J., Lott, L., & Glenn, S. H. (1993). *Positive discipline in the classroom: How to effectively use class meetings and other positive discipline strategies.* Rocklin, CA: Prima Publishing.

Nelson, J. R., Roberts, M. L., Mathur, S. E., & Rutherford, R. B. (1999). Has public policy exceeded our knowledge base? A review of the functional behavioral assessment literature. *Behavioral Disorders, 24,* 169–179.

Nelson, C. M., Scott, T. M., & Polsgrove, L. (1999). Perspective on educational/behavioral disorders: Assumptions and their implications for educational treatment. In L.M. Bullock and R.A. Gable (Eds.), *Third CCBD mini library services–What works for children and youth with E/BD: Linking yesterday and today with tomorrow.* Reston, VA: Interventional Council for Exceptional Children.

Nichols, P. (2001). Role of cognition and affect in functional and behavioral analysis. *Exceptional Children, 66,* 393–402.

Olson, J. L., & Platt, J. M. (2000). *Teaching children and adolescents with special needs* (3rd ed.). Upper Saddle River, NJ: Merrill.

OSEP Technical Assistance Center on Positive Behavioral Interventions and Supports. *Positive behavioral interventions and supports.* Accessed at http://pbis.org on July 21, 2008.

Panico, A. (1999). *Discipline and the classroom community: Recapturing control of our schools.* Mequon, WI: Stylex Publishing Co., Inc.

Payne, R. (2001). *A framework for understanding poverty.* Highlands, TX: aha! Process, Inc.

Perlstein, R., & Thrall, G. (1996). *Ready-to-use conflict resolution activities for secondary students.* Paramus, NJ: Center for Applied Research in Education.

Quinn, M. M., Gable, R. A., Fox, J., Rutherford, R. B. Jr., Van Acker, R., & Conroy, M. (2001). Putting quality functional assessment into practice in schools: A research agenda on behalf of E/BD students. *Education and Treatment of Children, 24*(3), 261–275.

Shores, R. E., & Wehby, J. H. (1999). Analyzing the classroom social behavior of students with EBD. *Behavioral Disorders, 7*(4), 194–199.

Sugai, G., Horner, R. H., & Sprague, J. R. (1999, May). Functional assessment-based behavior support planning: Research to practice to research. *Behavioral Disorders, 24*(3), 253–258.

Teach with movies: A unique tool for teachers and parents (2008). Accessed at www.teachwithmovies.org on July 21, 2008.

Van Acker, R. (1998). Dealing effectively with students who present behavior problems: The functional assessment of behavior. *Functional Assessment of Behavior Workbook.* Chicago, IL: Van Acker and Associates.

Van Acker, R., Boreson, L., Gable, R. A., & Potterton, T. (2005, March). Are we on the right course? Lessons learned about current FBA/BIP practices in schools. *Journal of Behavioral Education, 14*(1), 35–56.

Williams, E. (2005). *The bully, the bullied and beyond.* Chapin, SC: YouthLight, Inc.

Yell, M. L. (1997, September). IDEA amendments of 1997: Implications for special and general education teachers, administrators, and teacher trainers. *Focus on Exceptional Children, 30*(1), 1–19.

Make the Most of Your Professional Development Investment

Let Solution Tree schedule time for you and your staff with leading practitioners in the areas of:

- **Professional Learning Communities** with Richard DuFour, Robert Eaker, Rebecca DuFour, and associates
- **Effective Schools** with associates of Larry Lezotte
- **Assessment *for* Learning** with Rick Stiggins and associates
- **Crisis Management and Response** with Cheri Lovre
- **Classroom Management** with Lee Canter and associates
- **Discipline With Dignity** with Richard Curwin and Allen Mendler
- **PASSport to Success** (parental involvement) with Vickie Burt
- **Peacemakers** (violence prevention) with Jeremy Shapiro

Additional presentations are available in the following areas:

- Youth at Risk Issues
- Bullying Prevention/Teasing and Harassment
- Team Building and Collaborative Teams
- Data Collection and Analysis
- Embracing Diversity
- Literacy Development
- Motivating Techniques for Staff and Students

Solution Tree

555 North Morton Street
Bloomington, IN 47404

(812) 336-7700 • (800) 733-6786 (toll free) • FAX (812) 336-7790

email: info@solution-tree.com

www.solution-tree.com

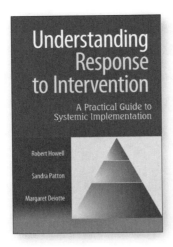

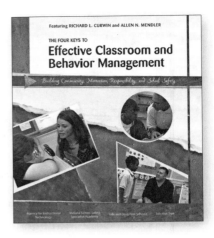

Understanding Response to Intervention: A Practical Guide to Systemic Implementation

Robert Howell, Sandra Patton, and Margaret Deiotte

Whether you want a basic understanding of RTI or desire thorough knowledge for district-level implementation, you need this book. Understand the nuts and bolts of RTI. Follow clear examples of effective practices that include systems and checklists to assess your RTI progress. **BKF253**

Pyramid Response to Intervention: RTI, Professional Learning Communities, and How to Respond When Kids Don't Learn

Austin Buffum, Mike Mattos, and Chris Weber, Foreword by Richard DuFour

Accessible language and compelling stories illustrate how RTI is most effective when built on the Professional Learning Communities at Work™ model. Written by award-winning educators, this book details three tiers of interventions—from basic to intensive—and includes implementation ideas. **BKF251**

The Four Keys to Effective Classroom and Behavior Management

Richard L. Curwin and Allen N. Mendler

Explore four skill areas essential to establishing a safe, supportive learning environment. In this video series, Curwin and Mendler demonstrate proven, research-based strategies in dramatized scenes and actual classroom settings. Deliver the material over a 2-day in-service period or in extended intervals. **VIF093**

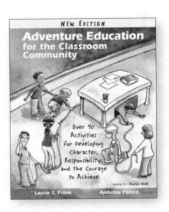

Creating Successful Inclusion Programs: Guidelines for Teachers and Administrators

Martin Henley

Gain specific strategies for creating and managing inclusive classrooms and guidelines for navigating the complicated legal and educational landscape of special education. This book includes historical information on special education and explores how inclusion programs fit in with the Individuals with Disabilities Education Act. **BKF151**

Discipline With Dignity for Challenging Youth

Allen N. Mendler and Richard L. Curwin

Create positive change in your most challenging students with the help of practical strategies found in this resource. The authors share proven practices for classroom discipline, reveal reasons why students misbehave, and offer 21 effective drug-free ways to help students with ADHD. **BKF229**

Adventure Education for the Classroom Community: Over 90 Activities for Developing Character, Responsibility, and the Courage to Achieve

Laurie S. Frank and Ambrose Panico

New edition! Engage your students in building a classroom community that supports character development, academic excellence, and individual and social responsibility. This character education curriculum is packed with activities that motivate students to choose positive behavior. **BKF221**

Solution Tree

Visit www.solution-tree.com or call 800.733.6786 to order.